Like a Bird on the Wing

by

Ian G. Macdonald

**Grosvenor House
Publishing Limited**

Ian G. Macdonald is hereby identified as author of this
work in accordance with Section 77 of the Copyright, Designs
and Patents Act 1988

The book cover picture is copyright to Ian G. Macdonald

This book is published by
Grosvenor House Publishing Ltd
28-30 High Street, Guildford, Surrey, GU1 3HY.
www.grosvenorhousepublishing.co.uk

A CIP record for this book
is available from the British Library

ISBN 978-1-906210-67-0

To all the staff at Portree High School
in memory of our late friend and colleague
Robert MacDonald

To Cathie & Paul

From your brother-in-law

Paul S MacDonald

Foreword

From my earliest days I was, and am, proud to be a Skyeman and I have taken a keen interest in the History, Culture, Landscape and Natural History of my native island, particularly the Trotternish area. This close association with Trotternish began on 8th January 1951 when I was born in the John Martin Memorial Maternity Hospital in Uig. This building is now the Uig Youth Hostel. Brought up in Portree, my family now live in Ollach in the Braes of Trotternish, on my great-grandfather's croft.

On the 8th of January 2006 I retired from the teaching profession after 33 years service. My final post was Depute Head Teacher at Portree High School where I had attended as a pupil from 1956 to 1969, returning as a teacher of Science and Guidance in 1980.

At the beginning of June 2006 I began to run tours of Trotternish for the Aros organisation based in Portree. The experience has been a most enjoyable one.

Acknowledgments

This booklet is not intended as an academic work, rather a collection of observations, tales, legends and history which I have picked up during my time on my native island. I hope that it will be a guide to some and a stimulus to all. For those who are interested in further study and more extensive works on the subjects touched on, I have included a list of some of the best books on Skye and related topics which will satisfy even the most demanding and studious.

I extend many thanks to those who have helped me with the booklet.

My former teachers at Portree High, George Moody, Alistair Turner, Forrest Moffat and especially the late Robin Murray who ran the School Field Club, which first gave me an insight into the wonderful scenery and wildlife that Skye has to offer. From these scientists and geographers I learned much of what appears in these pages.

Several of the stories and historical details were passed on to me by Donald MacDonald of Aros who has a wealth of knowledge of his home territory. My thanks go to Donald and all the staff at Aros who have made me very welcome.

"*Old Skye Tales: Traditions, Reflections and Memories*" by William MacKenzie and Jonathan MacDonald's "*Discovering Skye*" have been very helpful but some of the stories I have included are different; I learned them as a boy and therefore have no means of verifying their accuracy.

No booklet or indeed article, about the Isle of Skye should be contemplated until one has read Derek Cooper's classic reference book *"Skye"*. Likewise "Skye" by Ann MacSween has helped me greatly.

Many thanks go to my former primary school teacher, Christine MacLean, for proofreading and correcting my spelling and punctuation and to Cailean Maclean for his encouragement and advice. Any further mistakes which remain are my own!

Finally, and most importantly, I acknowledge with gratitude the superlative beauty of the landscape through which we travel. Even when the weather is indifferent, the views are sometimes astounding. Having myself travelled widely in Europe, I know of nowhere else with such appealing topography. When we park at the viewpoint at Rigg, and passengers from all parts of the World gasp with astonishment at the vista before them, I am reminded that we should indeed be grateful, not only for our wonderful surroundings but for the health and capacity, both physical and mental, to enjoy them.

I G M

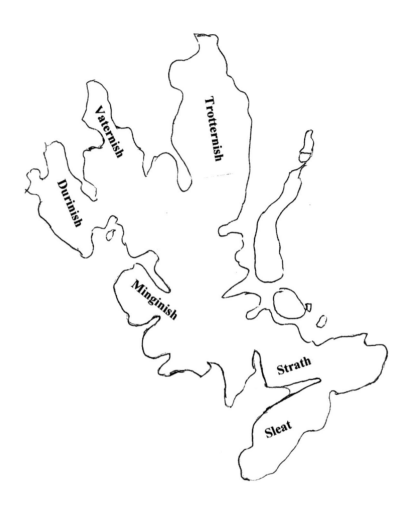

The Isle of Skye

CHAPTER 1

Perhaps the most commonly known name for the Isle of Skye is "The Misty Isle", *Eilean a Cheo,* but another title, and perhaps an older one (Dean Munro 1549), is "The Winged Isle".

*"The iyle is callit by the Erishe, Ellan Skyane, that is to say
in English, the Wingitt ile, by reason it has maney wyngs
and points lyand furth frae it thro the devyding of thir lochs."*

The first name of this island, noted by the Roman cartographer Ptolemy, in his early map, was *Scetis* and the Norse called it *Scaia.* The historian Adamnan in his *Life of St Columba* writing in 700 AD refers to Skye as Scia. This could mean either Cloud Island or Island of Wings.

On looking at a map, it appears that Skye is indeed composed of several wings. Trotternish, Vaternish, Durinish and Minginish were so named by the norsemen; the *-ish* ending meaning a headland or indeed a wing.

Our most famous Gaelic poet of the 20th Century, the late Dr. Sorley Maclean, describes Skye as the "big bird of Scotland, spreading its wings around Loch Snizort and around the World".

*"Do sgiathan aoibhneach air an sgaoileadh
Mu Loch Shnigheasort is mun t-saoghal"*

The reference to Loch Snizort, our largest fjord, is obvious, as it is positioned between the 'wings'; but 'spreading around the World' in this context, refers to the many Skye people who were forced to emigrate to all parts of the World due to the economic circumstances of the 19th Century and to the greed of their landlords.

It is our intention to explore the north easterly wing of Skye namely

Trotternish.—Thronda's Headland

Trotternish consists of "*The Braes of Trotternish*" immediately south of Portree and "*Iochdar Trotternish*" to the north of the capital. The most southerly point of Trotternish is the headland of *Mol*.

The original name of Portree Bay was Loch Chaluim Chille or St. Columba's Loch. The famous Irish saint came here in the year 585AD bringing Christianity to this part of the north and west of Scotland. Having founded the monastery of Iona in 563AD, he, and various other Irish monks, among them Maol Luag, Bishop of Lismore (Kilmaluag), Talorgan (Kiltaraglen) and Martin (Kilmartin), came to north Skye, setting up various daughter monasteries to the principal one at Iona. In the parishes of Kilmuir, Portree and Snizort there are some thirty remains of places of worship founded by these Irish monks. (Kil- means chapel or monk's cell). In Portree Bay itself there is a St. Columba Island with its ruined chapel. The significance of many of these religious remains being on small islands lies in the vow of monasticism taken by the monks. Columba's declared motive for coming to Scotland was to become an 'exile for Christ' and much of his time would have been spent in prayer and fasting.

The little village on the north side of St.Columba's Loch was known as Kiltaraglen until the year 1540.

Saint Columba, Abbot of Iona, born at Garten, County Donegal, Ireland in 521, visited Skye around 585. He belonged to Clan O'Donnell, and was of royal descent. His father's name was Fedhlimdh and his mother Eithne. He was given the baptismal name *Colum* meaning 'dove', but the manner of his early life meant that he was regarded as *Crimthan* meaning 'wolf'. He was afterwards known as *Colum-cille*, 'the dove of the churches' with regard to the many which he had set up. He is most closely associated with the north of Skye where most of the little chapels are on islets, either in sea lochs, freshwater lochs or indeed a river.

CHAPTER 2

Close to the town lies the area known as
 Sgoirebreac or **Scorrybreak** (The Steep Speckled Hill)
The rocks are indeed speckled hereabouts due to common white lichens including (*Parmelia saxatilis*),
 indicators of a relatively pollution-free atmosphere.
These were the Clan lands of the Nicolsons of *Sgoirebreac* (oldest of the Skye clans).

It is believed that the Nicolson or MacNicol clan were given these lands rent free by one of Scotland's earliest kings, Malcolm Can Mor (942 to 954), in recognition of their saving a herd of his cattle from the Norsemen in his native county of Sutherland.

This area extends north from Portree past the Storr lochs and Lealt. At Toravaig, the ancient seat of the chief, who played host to King James (V) in 1540, is now marked only by a cairn. The 17th Chief (Norman), saddled with debts, sold up his lands to Lord Macdonald in 1837, following two disastrous harvests and, along with a hundred or so of the clan, left Skye for Tasmania where his family still live. Most of the remnants of his clan were cleared from the land to make way for sheep farms. The lintel of the old *Sgoirebreac* house forms the fireplace of the present chief's Australian home.

In 1993, following a series of Clan Nicolson Gatherings from around the World, a monument was erected overlooking Portree Harbour. Nicolsons from all around the World have contributed to the purchase of this small part of their former clan lands.

Portree, we believe, took its name, *The King's Port* or *The King's Harbour,* from the visit of King James (V) of Scotland to Skye in 1540 in order to gain the allegiance of the clan chiefs.

Behind the Black Rock at the mouth of the bay, is the King's landing place *Creag na Mor Sluagh*. This title, 'The rock of the Multitude' gives weight to the historical fact that King James travelled with a large army and fleet, under the command of Alexander Lindsay, in order to exert his authority over the chiefs. It is related how the tents of the King and of his nobles and knights were ranged on the slopes surrounding the harbour, brightened by the pennons of the lances planted by every pavilion. The whole pageant was seen against the background of native woodland which surrounded the bay. The visit, marked by a considerable number of hangings of individuals judged to be unruly, seems to have had the desired effect.

The entrance to Portree Bay was described by the well known geologist, Hugh Miller, as "singularly majestic – the cliffs tower high on either side in graceful magnificence ... a palace gateway."

High on the hillside can be seen MacCoitar's Cave. MacCoitar was a robber in the pirate mould, whose men preyed on ships entering the harbour. In later days, in time of war, this spot, Battery Green, was equipped with big guns for harbour protection. Nowadays we can see one of the many salmon farms which have sprouted around our coasts. On the south shore is Camus Ban, one of the few sandy beaches in Skye. Near here are the ruins of the former community of Scorr, finally evacuated in 1905.

The White-tailed Eagle

Scorrybreak is the best spot for sighting the Sea Eagles which nest nearby. The Gaelic name for these birds is particularly evocative; *Iolaire suil na greine* (the eagle with the sun-lit eye).

Sea Eagles were once common in the Highlands but were killed off in the 19th Century due to their supposed threat to lambs, grouse and other game-birds. Re-introduced to the Islands of Rum in 1975, and Mull in 1985, several pairs now nest in Skye. These birds are the fourth largest birds of prey in the World and can have a wingspan of up to 7 feet (2.4m). The Sea Eagle Exhibition at Aros is well worth a visit, as it allows views of young eagles in the eyrie via a nest cam. Sea Eagles were revered by Neolithic people, and eagle skeletons have been found in Bronze Age burial chambers. Buzzards are also a common sight above *Ben Chracaig*, as several pairs nest on the nearby crags.

Also to be seen are ravens, rooks, and hooded crows.

The hooded crow is a sub-species of the carrion crow. Having a grey back and breast, its black head is hood-like. It is commoner in these parts than its all black cousin. There is a large and noisy rookery on the Meall overlooking the harbour. On fine evenings the raucous return of flocks to roost often provides an interesting spectacle. Herons are common, as they nest on the tall pine trees in the grounds of Viewfield House and behind the Aros Centre. On the track around the bay you will pass several species of tree; the hazel (*calltainn*), the oak (*darach*), birch (*beithe*), willow *(seileach)* and rowan *(caorann)*.

Trees are of great interest in the origins of the Gaelic language and culture. Derived from an earlier alphabet called *Ogam*, which consisted of a series of strokes to the left and right of a centre line, or corner on a stone pillar, Gaelic is based on the Latin alphabet. Each of the eighteen letters is named from a tree or plant, having it as initial. So A is called *Ailm* (Elm), B is *Beith* (Birch), C is *Coll* (Hazel), and so on. Trees have always had powerful associations in celtic mythology and culture. The Gaelic Alphabet trail at the Aros Centre is a good place to learn more about this interesting subject.

It is now hard to believe that Skye, until the 18th century, was heavily wooded. Nowadays, most of the island appears denuded of trees because they were used as fuel by the large population in the early 19th century, and then kept from regenerating by the predation of sheep. Sheep and trees do not co-exist comfortably. Most of Skye's native woodland is to be found on steep slopes and gullies where the trees cannot be reached. Returning from the Black Rock you will pass The

Cuillin Hills Hotel, at one time one of Lord MacDonald's hunting lodges. Now it is a lovely setting for weddings and the all-important photographs.

Travelling north out of Portree, you will see two of the many duns or hill forts which are so prevalent on the island, *Dun Torvaig* and *Dun Gerishader*. *Dun Gerishader*, close to the road, once had walls 14 feet thick. These protective hill forts were built in Neolithic times and afforded safety, for humans and their domestic animals, from invaders. Some of the forts were used mainly as signalling promontories for beacons to call the clans to arms, while others, known as brochs, were double walled and well protected. Each dun was built within sight of several others so that messages could be passed swiftly across the island. Over hundreds of years, much of the stone has been removed for the building of local housing. The best example of a broch in Skye is *Dun Beag* at Struan near Dunvegan. The brochs at Glenelg, on the mainland, and at *Dun Carloway*, on the Isle of Lewis, are also well worth a visit, as they are well preserved.

Although hunter-gatherers had passed through this area before, it is thought that it was in Neolithic times that farming and settlement first occurred. The Picts, with their ability in stone structure, were among the first. From about 800BC the Celtic people began to arrive and settle. They are believed to have come from mainland Europe, the area around the Rhine, Rhone and Danube. The Celtic language is divided into two main branches; Brythonic and Goidelic. Present day Welsh, Breton and Cornish come from the former and Scottish, Irish and Manx Gaelic from the latter.

In recent years there has been a resurgence of interest and popularity in Celtic art, design and music.

Some hundreds of years after the first Celts settled in Skye, the Viking 'summer raiders' began to create havoc with these settlements around our bays and lochs. Eventually these Norsemen also began to see the advantages of settling down in this area. Each of these peoples brought their own skills, knowledge and beliefs which became intertwined in the population.

CHAPTER 3

The Trotternish Ridge

The backbone of the Trotternish peninsula is a continuous ridge of rock more than 18 miles long which runs from south to north. Composed, along its regular height of 2000 feet, of the volcanic igneous rock called basalt, this is the longest such escarpment in Britain. There are gentle slopes to the west and steep scarp slopes along the eastern side of the ridge forming so-called "trap landscape". These giant landslips and rock falls are due to the presence of underlying layers of softer sedimentary rock which are affected by weathering, making the basalt ridge unstable. All around the east of Trotternish there is evidence of the effects of this dynamic landscape.

The Storr Lochs (*Loch Fada and Loch Leathann*)
Loch Fada was once the home of a mythical waterhorse which would wander abroad at night eating the crops. It was eventually despatched with a knife of pure iron.

These lochs now provide Portree's water supply, are excellent for brown and rainbow trout fishing and also act as storage for a Hydro-Electric power scheme which can provide a significant percentage of Skye's electrical energy requirements (7million units per year). Built in 1952, the dam and power-house feed electricity into the National Grid. The water plummets 150 metres down towards the sea to turn three turbines which can each generate 800Kw. The Lochs *Fada* (long) and *Leathann* (broad) are fed by a multitude of streams from the ridge which leads up to "The Storr" or *Fiocaill Storrach* (buck's molar tooth) 2358ft. "The Storr" is the mountain!

The sharp pinnacle, "The Old Man of Storr" is 165ft high, and a well known sea-mark, visible from 15 miles to the south, and was first climbed in 1955 by famous mountaineers Don Whillans and James Barber.

From the lochs here, in 1746, two lads carried a small boat to the sea-side to ferry Bonnie Prince Charlie to a degree of safety in the Island of Raasay. He remained there for only one night, however, as the soldiers of the Duke of Cumberland, in retaliation for the MacLeod of Raasay joining the Prince's cause, had burned all the houses as they rampaged across the Highlands in the wake of the battle of Culloden.

Of the modern-day boats maintained by the local Angling Association, it is interesting to note that one is specially adapted to take a wheelchair. This facility is proving very popular, as angling attracts locals and visitors alike to the Storr Lochs. Day passes for boat or bank are available.

In recent years there has been debate about the use of natural resources to provide electricity. This particular hydro-electric scheme is unobtrusive and provides power in a clean carbon-free manner. With lots of rainfall, strong winds, waves and tides around the coast, Skye is ideally placed to provide "green" energy. If our politicians were a little more willing "to grasp the nettle" we could easily be self-sufficient in pollution-free electricity in this island and indeed in Scotland. The arguments for and against wind-farms continue but there is room for compromise. Discrete schemes with a small number of turbines, sensitively sited, would benefit islanders and a mix of energy sources is surely the way forward.

In the late 1960s, Robin Murray, science teacher at the high school, set up a rain gauge at 2000ft on the Storr slopes, in order to monitor and compare rainfall here with his own, sea-level gauge at Prabost, 3 miles to the east. As expected, the rain bearing, prevailing southwest wind deposited considerably more moisture at this level.

The Bride's Veil waterfall - (so named because of its shape when in spate).

By the side of the road, for much of the summer, can be seen an interesting selection of wild flowers. Several varieties of *buttercup* grow beside some excellent examples of *ragged robin, eyebright* and *lousewort*.

Just up from the car park there is a clump of *blaeberry* which has very juicy fruits in August. This native plant is closely related to the *American Blueberry*, rich in vitamin C and antioxidants.

From here we see a couple of peat-stacks. Peat, dug from the ground in late spring, was once the main winter fuel for the Skye houses but is now only cut by a few enthusiasts or romantics.

The smell of peat-smoke is indeed lovely in small quantity. When the 'black-houses' were pervaded with it I'm sure the romance, as well as the visibility, was somewhat dimmed. Most of us have now joined the modern trend with our electric or oil-fired central heating. The commercial cutting of peat in the Highlands for gardening purposes is now frowned upon for environmental reasons, but the very small quantities now cut for domestic consumption and for the whisky industry has little negative effect.

The forestry on the slopes of the Storr is publicly owned and the network of paths is maintained by the Highland Council. In spring and autumn the changing colours of the larch trees produce an interesting contrast with their neighbouring evergreens. On the right of the road, the small plantation of Sitka spruce and lodge pole pine is commercial woodland destined for the pulp, paper and fibreboard industries. Both areas, although planted in the 1960s by the Forestry Commission, have been sold on. Much of the Commission's planting in the 21st Century no longer consists of rectangular blocks of "foreign" coniferous trees, but more natural, irregular copses of "native" woodland. With luck, you will spot a roe deer popping its head out of the woodland. Both roe and red deer are more common in the north of Skye than in the recent past as the number of sheep on the hill has declined. Along with the decline in government support for the sheep industry, the low price of wool has been an important factor in sheep production becoming less economic.

CHAPTER 4

Bearreraig Bay

Below the Storr Lochs, on the seashore is the Power Station at Bearreraig Bay. A walkway with 674 steps leads down to it but, as these have recently become unsafe, visitors to the bay are encouraged to use the newly constructed path. The geology of this area is particularly interesting. Below the igneous basalt layers are softer sedimentary deposits which include sandstones, limestones and shales. There are even a couple of thin seams of coal. In the limestone rocks on the shore of the easterly bays some very fine examples of fossils of the Jurassic period are to be found. Oysters, scallops, ammonites and belemnites are the commonest present, along with occasional trilobites, but in the mid 1960s Norrie Gillies, the power station manager, discovered a fossil ichthyosaurus.

Ten feet long with 21 vertebrae, it is the finest sample found in this country. This creature was a marine reptile similar to our modern-day dolphin. Today, this fossil can be seen at the Environmental Centre at Broadford.

The first dinosaur bone to be found in Scotland was chanced upon at Bearreraig as recently as 1997. This fossil find was part of an 'arm' bone of the stegosaurus, the oldest ever such stegosaurus bone discovered in the World. Fully grown, this creature would have been 15 metres long. Bearreraig is recognised as one of the most interesting Jurassic exposures in the UK. This fossil is kept at the Ellishader Museum.

In 1993 cetiosaurus footprints were discovered just up the coast at Staffin Bay, as were those of hardrosaurs and several examples from coelophysis – a meat-eating miniature dinosaur no bigger than a medium sized dog.

At the edge of the bay can be seen the remains of the gable end of a salmon fishing station. It is hard to believe that this area had a large population up until the early 1800s. In 1837 around 500 people emigrated to Australia from around here, with hundreds more going to North America before the close of the century. In the early 1900s, a hoard of silver coins, brooches, bracelets and rings was found near this spot. There were 100 tenth century Anglo Saxon silver pennies and 18 coins minted in Samarkand.

An enormous rock on the shore hereabouts is called *An Eaglais Bhreagach* (false kirk) because of its resemblance to a church. Here, the legendary MacCuien performed the rite of Taighairm which involved the roasting of cats to raise the Devil. He would not have been welcome at SSPCA headquarters!

The surname MacCuien is an interesting one, different from MacQueen, although the Gaelic for both names has a similar spelling and pronunciation. The modern version of the name is MacCowan (of Highland Toffee fame!), but many of that clan changed their names to MacDonald, either to show allegiance to Lord MacDonald, the feudal superior, or to avoid the notoriety the name had acquired. My own great-great-grandfather Finlay MacCuien and his wife Catherine in the 1841 National Census, had changed surnames to MacDonald by 1851.

The car park beneath the Old Man of Storr, and its overflow, are nearly always full throughout the holiday season, which now stretches from March to late October. On average, a total of 30,000 visitors per year are prepared to walk up to the base of the pinnacle in all weathers. This is three times Skye's present population of just a little over 10,000! Very few of these walkers will be residents, as human nature dictates that having a beauty spot close to home results in us ignoring it!

In 1841 the population of the island reached its peak of 23,082, declining thereafter to a low of 7183 in 1971, but has stabilised, and indeed risen in recent years.

The depopulation of many of Skye's glens to provide pasture for the *caoraich mhor,* the cheviot sheep, has been well documented. From the mid 1700s, families were forced to leave Skye due to economic circumstances. When the people were no longer required as warriors for the chief, or labour for the kelp industry, the landowners encouraged their departure to southern cities or to the colonies. Renting out land for the gentry to hunt and fish became more lucrative for the chiefs of MacDonald and MacLeod. It has been estimated that, between 1770 and 1900, a total of 6940 **families** left the island (perhaps 35,000 individuals)!

Skye also contributed 10,000 common soldiers, 600 captains and many other higher ranking officers to the Napoleonic wars!

The eviction of Norman Nicolson, *Tormad Scorrybreac,* the 17th clan chief, in 1837, illustrates well the sadness of final departure from a much-loved homeland. The Nicolson debt to Lord MacDonald had gradually built up as the clan was confined to a smaller holding. Norman no longer had the freedom to hunt and fish for food on his native hills. His uncle *Padruig Mor* judiciously became gamekeeper for Lord MacDonald's deer-forest and indeed, some of his descendants still live in Trotternish, but Norman persisted in taking deer and salmon until the final edict came from Edinburgh banishing him from the estate. He and his people finally left for Tasmania. In his bitterness he composed this song:

'S gann gu'n dirich mi chaoidh,	It's unlikely that I will ever climb
Dh'ionnsuidh frith ard	again to the high forest of the
a'mhunaidh,	hills.
'Sgann gu'n dirich mi chaoidh,	It is unlikely, etc.
Tha mo ghunna caol air	My slender gun has rested, and
meirgeadh,	I will never hunt with it again.
Cha teid mi do'n t-seilg les tuille.	It is unlikely, etc.
'S gann, etc.	

Thug na h-uachdrain uiann le ceilg,	The landlords took by guile the
An t-saorsa sheilg bh'againn uile.	hunting rights that we all had.
'S gann, etc	It is unlikely, etc.
Cul mo laimh ri laghan fiar,	The back of my hand to unjust
Tha toirmeasg biadh thug	laws that forbid the food that
Dia do'n duine.	God gave man.
'S gann, etc.	It is unlikely, etc.

As we drive past the end of the coniferous woodland beneath the Storr, a wonderful vista opens out to our right. The islands of Rona, Raasay and Fladda appear in the foreground with the mountains of Torridon and Applecross, on the Scottish mainland as a backdrop.

Close to the main road is *Slochd a'Cheannaiche* (the hollow of the Packman) who was murdered by two robbers.

Chuir mi bhiodag anns a' bhodach
's leig am bodach ran as;
Chuir mi leis a chreag e,
's theich mi leis a mhàileid.

A young lad was witness to this event but they put him in such a state of fear that he promised never to tell a living soul. When he escaped and crossed the hills to Snizort, he ended up at the manse door of the Rev. MacQueen. The shrewd minister, realising the lad's difficulty, advised him to tell his tale to a large rock rather than a living soul! The murderers were soon apprehended and duly convicted. One culprit, Angus Buchanan was hanged at the Meall in Portree on 18th June 1742, "with the greatest decency and without the least disturbance". His accomplice, Duncan MacQueen, was similarly hanged at the Gallowmuir near Inverness, both sentences acting as a warning to others across the county.

Rigg Viewpoint

From here we look across to the islands of Raasay, Fladda, Eilean Tigh and Rona, and to the mainland near Gairloch. The

Ross-shire mountains, composed of torridonian sandstone, often reflect the sunshine in an eye-catching manner. To the south is the tiny island of Holm, a well known fishing marker, from the days when the Sound of Raasay was an area rich in haddock, cod and ling. Most of the local boats now go after shellfish. Prawns, langoustines, crabs and lobsters are the main catch and most go to the discerning tables of Europe.

Below us are the flat fertile fields of Rigg, now deserted, but once the crofts of sixty families evicted in the early 19th century and forced to sail for the Carolinas and Canada. Some of the old sad songs, written by men of the area as they turned for a last look at the shores of their birthplace, are still sung at ceilidhs, both here and in Cape Breton, Nova Scotia. In living memory there has been only one burial in the ancient Rigg cemetery as the MacDonald land owners had stopped intern-ments here during the 19th century, forcing the Nicolsons to carry their dead across the hills. At each of the resting places where the coffins were laid down, a few stones would be added to a cairn. The occupants of the Rigg townships were crofters and fishermen; witness the natural jetty; but this coast is very unsafe in stormy weather.

A very different mode of transport is used by the ladies who cook and clean for the occupants of the naval base at the north of Rona these days! They travel to work by helicopter from the base at Kyle of Lochalsh.

Like all lighthouses in the UK, the Rona one is now auto-matic. One of the last keepers to serve here was Calum MacLeod of Arnish, Raasay, who is well known as the builder of Calum's Road.

The reason for the naval base in these airts is because imme-diately north of Rona is the deepest sea depth on the European continental shelf. This results in much activity by N.A.T.O. submarines and aircraft.

The ruins of a salmon fishers' bothy can be seen beside the natural harbour. In the 1880s, eighty eight men were employed from May to October between Portree and Staffin fishing for the wild Atlantic salmon by a method known as bag-netting. They lived in bothies along the coast during the week, returning home at weekends. By law, the bag-nets were required to be left open on Sundays so that the fish could swim freely through them. Very large catches were common on this coast and around Raasay. The fish were stored in the Portree ice-house before being transported south. Salmon fishing remained profitable in this area until the 1970s. Few wild salmon are caught these days, due, probably, to over-fishing in the Atlantic, but this industry has been replaced by salmon farming. Many thousand tonnes of farmed Skye salmon are exported annually. Unfortunately, all of Scotland's salmon farming companies have been bought over by the Norwegians. The Vikings are still at their old games!

As we travel past the former townships of Holm, Rigg, Tote and Lealt, we see the signs of former cultivation by the method known as *feannagan*, lazybeds or rigs. The thin soil was ridged up to help with cropping and drainage. Cultivation was achieved using the *Cas Chrom* or foot plough.

To increase fertility, seaweed was hauled from the shore in creels, chiefly by the women. The system of allocation of the strips of land was known as the run-rig system. Each family took part in a ballot which ensured that the system was fair. If you had a poor strip of land in year one, you might be more fortunate in year two. However, such a system did not lend itself to land improvement, as there was little incentive for a family to increase the fertility of a patch which would next year go to a neighbour.

It was a characteristic of those times however, that the poor and aged were not forgotten by the community. Portions of land called *cionagan nam bochd* were set aside for those not capable of tilling the soil. These areas were cultivated by friends and neighbours.

It is interesting that our local, now international, Gaelic Rock Band, Runrig, has taken its name from this system of land use. At least five of the original band members were pupils of

Portree High School. The late Robert MacDonald, their accordionist, lived up the road at Valtos. Former band member, Donnie Munro, now a solo artiste, occupies the modern-day successor to the old Scorrybreak House.

Two of the many seaweeds which grow on the rocks in the sea at Rigg are *mathar an duileisg* (mother of dulse) from which carrageen pudding is made, and dulse itself, (*cal duileasg*), which makes a very nourishing soup. People from the Snizort area would think nothing of making a journey across the ridge to gather dulse at Rigg. Dulse is rich in iodine, a mineral necessary for the healthy operation of the thyroid gland, and it was highly regarded in ancient times as "a sweetener of the blood". In Skye homes, dulse was often served as a vegetable, cooked as one would cabbage.

CHAPTER 5

Invertote Carpark

The township of Lealt is so called from the Gaelic meaning half-stream, as the crofts are situated on only one of the two tributaries which join to form the Tote river before it crashes over a spectacular waterfall.

There was once a school built here but, as the population dropped before it was occupied, it was carried away, stone by stone and rebuilt at Valtos.

The most prominent peak on the Trotternish ridge to be seen from here is *Sgurr a Mhadaidh Ruaidh* (The Hill of the Red Fox). Indeed foxes are very common on these hills. In 1774 the land-lords imposed a tax of 'fox money' on their tenants. The money was collected along with the rent and then shared out at the year's end to those who could show that they had killed foxes. Fox tails were the evidence. In 1765 a total of 119 foxes were killed in Trotternish alone. The last Skye wolf was killed in 1742.

Beneath this hill is *Loch Cuithir* from which, from 1886 diatomite was mined. Diatomite, or to give it its German name, Kieselghur, is a mineral substance formed from the body-casings of millions of tiny diatoms or unicellular algae (*bacillario-phyceae*) found in both freshwater and marine environments. Raw diatomite is off-white or tan coloured powder with a multitude of uses from face powders, beer and wine filters to electrical insulation. Because of its high silica content, it is a mild abrasive and so is effective in toothpaste and metal polishes, soaps and detergents. Being natural, it is a more acceptable alternative to bleach, or other abrasive chemicals, which can cause problems to humans and the environment. A railway was built in 1887 to carry tons of this mineral to a drying station, the ruins of which can be seen on the shore below the cliffs. It was then exported by ship to factories in the main industrial centres.

The railway closed in 1915 when men left at the start of the First World War and the line was dismantled in 1920. In 1930, and again in the early 1960s, there were attempts to revive the industry. Drying and storage sheds were built at Uig, but the attempts proved uneconomic. Skye lochs hold only 0.1% of the world reserves but those in Lochs Cuithir and Loch Vallerain near Digg are amongst the purest. In Loch Cuithir about 350,000 metric tonnes of diatomite remain, but Loch Sneosdal in Kilmuir has as much as one million metric tonnes remaining. An English couple, who travelled with us on one of the Aros tours, were able to tell me that they had witnessed extraction of diatomite in Iceland during their holiday in 2005.

It is interesting to note that, in the sixties, the diatomite firm employed a timekeeper who came to live on Skye and took a great liking to the area which provided him, the author Alan Campbell MacLean, with the setting for several of his inspirational adventure story books for teenagers: *"The Hill of the Red Fox"*, *"The Year of the Stranger"* and *"Master of Morgana"*. The swing bridge, now washed away, which led to the salmon fishers' bothy on the shore, was crucial to the plots in more than one of the books. The *"Master of Morgana"* also featured a German submarine and, it is believed locally, that MacLean got his idea from a tale that U-boats secretly and regularly put in to Invertote for fresh water supplies during World War II. No doubt the tale grew out of the fact that the pre-war operator of the Diatomite works was Herr Blondell. Though German, he was not interned and there was local suspicion that he operated a clandestine radio.

Another two of MacLean's books, *"Ribbon of Fire"* and its sequel *"The Sound of Trumpets"* are set at the time of the clearances and features Sheriff Ivory, the lairds, factors, ground-officers and sheriff-officers who made trouble for the local crofters.

Culnancnoc (back of the hills)
When an emigrant ship sailed to America in 1847 with a large number of the people from here, one woman shed bitter tears and said: *"Cha b'e cul nan cnoc ach aghaidh na greine"*, It was not 'back of the hills' but the face of the sun.

Lonfearn (the stream of the alders)
This area was also granted to the Nicolson clan in the distant past to be held in perpetuity "while a wave breaks on the shore and a black cow gives white milk". It had been a place of worship in pre-Christian times. Oak and alder trees were sacred to the ancient Celtic people and perhaps there were once alder groves hereabouts. The remains of a number of beehive dwellings are still in evidence. It is thought they were once inhabited by the wise men, priests or judges of the ancient Celts. The local name for them is *Tighean Druineach* (Druids' Houses).

Valtos

The natural promontory on which Dun Dearg dominated the area at one time is composed of vertical pillars of basalt rock. Indeed the name of this wider district *Staffin* means 'the place of the rock pillars'. The Island of Staffa in southwest Scotland has the same name-root and the same geology. Fingal's Cave, made famous by Mendelson's music, *The Hebrides Overture*, is formed from basalt pillars, as is the Giant's Causeway in the north of Ireland.

As we pass Dun Dearg, both the igneous pillars and the weathering of the softer sedimentary sandstone are so obvious, that the reasons for the fallen basalt columns on the shoreline below are clear even to the non-geologist.

Dun Dearg was once known as a beacon point for calling the clans to arms.

Valtos was the home of Norman Stewart, *Tormod Choinnich* (known locally as Parnell, after his Irish counterpart). He led a protest against the unjust rent rises, and subsequent threats of eviction, following a revaluation of land on the Kilmuir estate in 1877. Refusal to pay the extra rent, by the crofters of Valtos and neighbouring Ellishader, led to eventual climbdown by the landowner and reduction of rents by a quarter. This brought a temporary peace in this part of Skye, but further trouble was brewing in the Braes of Trotternish. Stewart and his neighbours were to give important evidence of the landlord injustices to the Napier Commission in 1883.

Does Valtos have any other claims to fame? Well yes; the first supertanker to dock in Britain, at Milford Haven in fact, was captained by a Valtos man!

Skye's first lemonade factory operated from here but the fizz soon went out of the project. Down the road at *Grealin*, meaning the sunny spot (where the sun always shines), an attempt was made to grow tobacco. Yes, you've guessed; it failed! Not so the efforts of the aforementioned, enterprising, Calum MacLeod of Raasay, however. He grew tobacco successfully at Arnish during World War II. It was smoked and enjoyed by the local bodaich, but Calum was a non-smoker.

Loch Mealt

Around the loch we see further examples of the remains of duns (Raisaburgh, Connavern and Grianan).

Loch Mealt is the only freshwater loch in Skye to have as inhabitants a species of pink-fleshed fish called Arctic Char. Believed to have bred here since the last ice-age, Arctic Char are found in Loch Lomond and Loch Tay in central Scotland. Although not popular with the Skye palate, these fish are regarded as a delicacy in parts of the world, notably Canada.

Eillishader, on the shores of Loch Mealt, has close associations with Ronald Selby Wright, founder of the Boys' Brigade movement. Likewise, Norman Drummond, former parish minister and leading light of the very successful Columba 1400, has his home here.

The Kilt Rock

The Kilt Rock is one of the best known geological features on the Isle of Skye and it is justly famous. Many of our guests are awestruck at its grandeur. The 19th century poet and novelist, Robert Buchanan, visiting in 1883, wrote "here is a panorama of cliff-scenery quite unmatched in Scotland. Towering into the air like the fretwork of some Gothic temple, roofless to the sky".

The vertical black basalt columns and horizontal strata on the cliffs give an effect similar to the pleats and patterns on the tartan of a kilt.

With a wintery northeasterly wind, the stream that forms the Mealt waterfall is often blown back and upwards over the little carpark, which in summertime is one of the busiest in Skye.

This is an interesting spot for wildflowers. In spring, the *lesser celendine, wood sorrel* and *water cress* are first to appear followed by *bladder campion, spotted orchid and bog cotton.*

In summer the purple *black knapweed* towers over the yellow *Creeping Cinquefoil* and *tormentil.*

Fragrant *meadowsweet* grows in clumps and was once used by Skye folk to make a tea known to reduce fever.

Nowadays, its natural analgesic and anti-inflamatory properties are recognised by a Skye company that advertises oil, lotion and soap remedies for joint and muscle pain. Many of these cures were known to, and used by, the Beaton or Bethune family in Skye and the other islands. *sneezewart* and *yarrow* are also to be found throughout the summer. It was thought that the ancient clan warriors used *yarrow* to control the bleeding from battle wounds. Another interesting plant, which flowers throughout the summer, is *sheep's bit scabious* which has both male and female flowers.

Here we can see examples of Scotland's three main types of heather. *calluna vulgaris,* ling heather, *erica cinerea,* the bell heather and *erica tetralix* the cross-leaved heath.

Another favourite plant is the *bog myrtle* with its attractive and strong scent. Interestingly, the sap of this plant is used to discourage the biting midges which plague us during the warmer months. Midges prove a major topic of conversation throughout the summer. It is rumoured that the Forestry Commission and Scottish Hydro Electric are issuing Avon Skin-So-Soft to their hunky workers because it is proving more effective than most midge-repellants!

In the early 1800s, the Rev. John MacCulloch, visiting Skye, described midges as "the torment of the country", "the light militia of the lower sky...with sharp teeth and ingenious snouts".

From August, other interesting plants to be found here, and in many other places around Trotternish, are the pleasant orange flowering *montbretia,* no doubt a garden escapee, and the pink opportunistic *rosebay willowherb,* which quickly colonises disturbed waste ground.

Sea birds there are in plenty. Fulmars nest on the cliffs and over the summer period it is interesting to note how quickly the fledglings become skilled flyers, using the updrafts from the cliffs to glide along with scarcely a wing beat.

Many of our visitors are keen to see puffins with their multi-coloured beaks but we, unfortunately, have to disappoint them. While puffins are known to nest on Eilean Trodday, we know of no nesting sites on Skye itself. We can often compensate, however, by pointing out black guillemots. They are interesting in that they have brilliantly red feet!

On the little shallow freshwater loch which leads to Loch Mealt we often see the little grebe and tufted duck. The velvety black coot with its distinctive white face breeds by the loch side. After only a few days of fishing by mum's side, the chicks become independent and dive frequently, with obvious enjoyment.

CHAPTER 6

The townships of Maligar, Marishader and Garros are to be seen across Loch Mealt. The placenames are interesting. Maliger comes from a Gaelic root *mall* – meaning rent and *guer* – meaning suet. The rent money in times past was originally asked for as a certain weight of sheep-fat. Marrishader has a Norse root meaning a summer pasture for mares. Garros means a narrow river mouth. At Garros there are two stone pillars commemorating the spot where two brothers fought to the death for an inheritance. We should indeed learn lessons from history!

The famous Martin family of Marishader, (a branch of which became the Martins of Bealach), had their ancestral home in this area. They are said to have taken their name from an ancient chapel dedicated to Saint Martin which is still to be seen in the present day cemetery at Clachan. Some historians have argued that this Martin was the famous French St. Martin of Tours, although it is highly unlikely that he visited Skye. It is more likely, as some others assent, that this St. Martin was a colleague of St. Columba. Many of the Martin family distinguished themselves in the medical and legal professions. The best known was Dr. Martin Martin, youngest son of Donald Martin of Bealach, educated at the University of Leiden in the Netherlands and tutor to both the families of MacDonald of Duntulm and MacLeod of Dunvegan. He wrote *"A Description of the Western Isles of Scotland"* in 1716. It became the classic travel volume of that era. The river which runs from here into Staffin Bay is known as the Kilmartin River, as it flows past the Kilmartin Cemetery, the last resting place of this clan.

Aonghas na Gaoithe was a Martin who married a Danish Princess Bernice and had seven sons. He is buried in Kilmuir Cemetery and we will refer to him, and some of his feats, again.

Beinn Edra

This is a prominent summit on the main Trotternish Ridge, literally meaning "the hill between them". In the closing days of World War II, in Spring 1945, it was the scene of a very sad accident. A Flying Fortress aircraft, belonging to the USA, with a crew of eight was lost when it collided with the mist-covered hill. The plane was on its way back to the States, via Prestwick and Iceland, and no doubt the men would have been in high spirits in anticipation of being reunited with their loved ones. As the recovered bodies of the airmen were carried back to the mainland for repatriation, the pupils of Portree High School stood to attention in poignant sympathy with our allies. Pieces of the twin-engine aircraft can still be seen on the mountain.

Ellishader Museum

This small museum shows examples of the fossils found in the area as well as agricultural implements used over the years. Open 10.30 am to 1pm except Wednesdays. The owner is a local man who was very involved in the interesting geological discoveries in recent years.

The Geology of Skye and Raasay is most interesting and attracts many students from a number of Universities on field trips.

The bulk of Skye is composed of horizontal, small-grained basalt layers formed from ancient igneous lava flows. Through these there are very hard intrusive dykes and sills of dolerite and peridotite. The Black Cuillins are composed of another type of igneous rock, with large grains, called gabbro. The Red Cuillins consist of a granite-like granophyre containing crystals of felsite and rhyolite.

Throughout Skye, beneath the ubiquitous basalt strata, there are layers of soft Jurassic sedimentary rock consisting of shales, limestones and sandstones. In the south of Skye, where the igneous intrusions meet the limestone, metamorphosis has occurred and the metamorphic rock, marble, has been formed. Skye Marble is famous throughout the World. Quarried at Torrin in South Skye for many years, its grey/green-veined slabs were used to build the high altar of Iona Abbey, the fireplace of Armadale Castle, and if some writers are to be believed, some features of the Palace of Versailles and the Vatican.

Much of the once horizontal and vertical strata has been faulted, twisted and weathered by ice and water to produce the varied landscape we see today.

Clachan

The present-day graveyard at Clachan is the subject of an interesting tale. More than two centuries ago the local people planned to build a new cemetery closer to the main centre of population at Garafad. They collected together a large quantity of stone to make a dyke for the new graveyard enclosure. One morning it was discovered that the prepared stone, along with the workmen's tools had disappeared. These were eventually discovered near the old Kilmartin site at Clachan. Some force had been at work in the community. Was it the fairies, or perhaps some local people doing a night-shift? Either way, the community accepted that their dead should be buried in the same place in which their ancestors had been interred over hundreds of years.

Churches

The Staffin area has four currently used church buildings, none of them as well attended as in former days, when this was a community particularly renowned as God-fearing. Although most church services are now conducted in English, there are still

Gaelic services with the beautiful and plaintive 'lining out'. The precentor chants each line of a Psalm for the congregation to repeat melodiously. Because so few Highlanders in the 18th and 19th Centuries, could read Gaelic, this system had become necessary. Recently, comparisons have been drawn to the singing style of Christian groups of African/American origin and suggestions made that they had learned from exiled Highlanders.

The first Christian missionary in these parts, St. Columba, is commemorated in the building known as **Columba 1400.**

This Columba Centre runs courses for youth groups from the city environment and is based on Christian principles, The young people enjoy an outward-bound experience with canoeing, sailing, hill-walking and climbing. Many have benefited from team-building and self-reliance exercises. One of our tour passengers on the Aros coach, on a particular occasion, told us that she had spent a week here with her Youth Club and the experience had "changed her life". She had come back to Skye on holiday with her boyfriend because the area had become so important to her.

Others who benefit from the Columba experience are stressed executives from large corporations and multi-nationals who enjoy the de-stressing and team-building. I notice that Head and Depute Head teachers from the Highland Council were represented in 2007. I trust their experience will benefit pupils!

The little bridge on the old road was built to the design of the famous engineer, Sir Thomas Telford, as is the Church of Scotland nearby. It will come as a surprise that there is also a third connection with Telford. A wrecked ship in Staffin Bay was called the Thomas Telford.

Telford, of course, built the main road through Skye from Kyleakin to Portree.

Staffin School

The Staffin School is one of 18 Primary schools on Skye. Approximately 80% of the pupils in this school learn through the medium of the Gaelic Language. Parents have the choice of English or Gaelic Medium education for their children. This recent development in Skye schools is helping to reverse the steep decline in numbers of Gaelic speakers and, along with the Gaelic College, *Sabhal Mor Ostaig* in south Skye, is producing a new vibrancy and self-confidence among the young people of the island. The help of peripatetic music teachers has also had a very positive effect. Many youngsters now learn to play the distinctive musical instruments so important in the culture. The *clarsach* (or highland harp), accordion, fiddle and, of course, the bagpipes are again being studied. Once more the sweet and sad sound of Gaelic song has returned to our communities.

CHAPTER 7

Staffin Pier

As we branch off right from the main road we pass through a small wood composed mainly of alder trees, down to the bridge across the Kilmartin River. Here we see the artificial pools and man-made weirs to entice the salmon to lie up where they may provide sport for the angler. Lord MacDonald had another of his Shooting and Fishing Lodges here from Victorian times but, following a spell as a Youth Hostel, it has been purchased recently by the Columba Foundation. A long stone dyke was built in the 19th century to separate the township land from the lodge. The *Garadh-fada* has now given its name to the area of Garafad. The MacQueen family had this township rent-free as long as they could supply MacDonald of the Isles with a large number of salmon each year. They were evicted when they failed to make up the required total!

By the riverside we see *marsh marigolds, primroses, scots' bluebells, buttercups, St. John's wort* and a number of *orchid* varieties among the hazel and ash trees.

St. John's wort was reckoned a charm against witchcraft and Skye women were known to put a flower at the bottom of their milk pail to discourage those who would put the evil eye on their milking cows. In Gaelic, this perennial herb is known as '*achlais Challum Chille*' or the armpit package of St. Columba, carried everywhere, for its many medicinal benefits.

The road passes over *Uamh na Calaman*, the Doves' cave, a nesting place for rock pigeons.

At *An Corran* is the shell midden which first gave an indication that Skye had human occupants as early as the Mesolithic age (middle stone age). Martin Wildgoose first recorded the rock shelter in 1988 enabling excavation to occur prior to roadworks in 1993. Until then, it was thought that Neolithic man were the earliest occupants of the island. Bones of the European Brown bear were found here, from a time when Skye was thought, not only to have been joined to mainland Scotland but also mainland Europe. Since then several other Mesolithic sites have been found across the island.

On the rocks exposed at very low tide are the footprints of coelophysis, diminutive dinosaurs. These dinosaurs were dog-size meat eaters.

Artificial otter holts were installed here during the road building operations, but the increased traffic flow has discouraged the creatures and they seem to have moved their residence across to Stenscholl island.

On the other side of Staffin Bay, in a large rock visible at low tide, a local man discovered a fossil pleiseosaur. The Hunterian Museum at Glasgow University was planning to extract it and float it out on barrels. They reckon that if left in position it will suffer damage. Like so many finds, it may go to a museum in the south of Scotland.

At the Staffin Pier, the now ruined store and the original pier structure were built by the Congested Districts Board in the late 1800s. The building of it gave work to lots of men in the community as they were required to use only stone from Stenscholl Island, although, as you will see, there is plenty suitable building stone all around.

The *Cadha Riathach* path was the only route by which stores and supplies could come into the community in the early 1900s. Packhorses were used to take goods to the six Staffin shops.

Gulls nest on the cliffs above. Mostly herring gulls, black-backed gulls and some fulmars. On the shore, the calling of the oyster catchers indicate that they are protecting their nests above the tide-line.

The local community is setting up an outdoor Eco-Museum in the pier area and throughout the district. There are remains of an Iron Age Fort nearby, although there is not much to see at present. There will, however, be a series of interpretive plaques to help us appreciate what the archaeologists have discovered.

To the south of the bay is a *Caraidh* or fish-trap. Up until the mid 20th century these were used, as the tide fell, to trap fish to feed the community.

At the back of Stenscholl Island is Whisky Creek *(Geodha an Uisge Bheatha)*. Grain from Kilmuir was shipped across to Gairloch on the mainland where whisky was distilled and smuggled back to Skye, traded for potatoes, and hidden here, to be distributed under cover of darkness. There was a tragedy at Brothers' Point further down the coast when two lads from south Skye were drowned while being pursued by the Customs' cutter.

Local mythology has it that Staffin Bay was formed by a violent storm. In this storm the Raasay chief, *Iain Garbh MacIlle Chalum* MacLeod, was returning by boat from the Island of Lewis. A local witch had guaranteed him good weather. As he and his men and hounds sailed off they enjoyed pleasant conditions while the witch gently swirled the water in her basin. She asked her young daughter to continue in this fashion. Teenagers then, as now, get bored easily so she began splashing the water. A violent storm blew up drowning *Iain Garbh* and his men and creating Staffin Bay. The hounds survived and clambered ashore at *Creag nan Con Glas* (the rock of the grey hounds), below the township of *Digg*.

There have, of course, been many sad accidents at sea on this dangerous coast. On 17 November 1893, a fishing boat from Achmelvich on the Sutherland mainland, and all its crew were lost when it foundered on rocks at Valtos – *Na Boghanan*. The bodies were found at *Port Earlais*. It is believed that it was this tragedy which inspired the song '*S daor a cheannach mi an t-iasgach*. (I paid a great price for following the fishing lifestyle).

CHAPTER 8

Stenscholl, on the main road, means 'field of stones', and indeed this is a very accurate description, as the houses and road are built on a raised beach, the present tide level being considerably below its original. The long, flat fields were well known for their crops of hay and corn. A very few crofters still make hay coils and corn stooks, as the plastic-wrapped silage bales are less weather-dependant, nowadays. They are not so visually pleasing however!

It is interesting to note that Norse and Gaelic placenames in Skye occur in equal numbers. The Viking invaders settled down in the islands of the west of Scotland, intermarrying with the local Celtic people and, indeed, these islands became part of the Norse empire from the year 1097 until 1266. Most modern Skye folk fall into one of two distinct body shapes: short, dark Celtic types or tall, blonde Viking types. The historian, Dr. Alistair MacLean, brother of Dr. Sorley MacLean the poet, gave a very interesting example to illustrate the origin of some common Skye surnames. "The names MacSween and MacSwan are both MacSuain in Gaelic. This clearly represents the son or family of Sven and indicates a definite Norse derivation. The MacQueens, on the other hand, are MacCuinn in Gaelic meaning the son of Conn, probably '*Conn of the hundred battles*', which suggests an Irish derivation and perhaps a common ancestor with the MacDonalds."

At the Battle of Largs in 1263, King Alexander III of Scotland defeated King *Haakon* of Norway. *Haakon*, who gave his name to the narrows between Skye and the mainland, Kyleakin, escaped to Orkney where he died of wounds

sustained in the battle. His successor, *Magnus* sued for peace.
At the Treaty of Perth in 1266 the Norsemen gave up all claims
to the Scottish Islands.

The Quiraing

The Quiraing (Round fold or pen) was reckoned a place of
safety for cattle. This is a most unusual weathered rock forma-
tion. It is said that 4000 head of cattle could be sheltered here
and looked after by a few young lads in time of trouble, while
the adult males fought off the invaders. There are giant pillars
and chasms, the needle, the prison and the table. The table is a
lush green area on which an annual midsummer shinty match
would take place in the old days. This walk was particularly
popular in Victorian times, with 50 to 60 visitors per day driving out from Portree to climb among these awesome rocks.
Today's visitors are no less enthusiastic. This area has become
popular as a backdrop for lots of television and cinema adver-
tisements, from Japanese cars to expensive perfumes.

The best views of the Quiraing are from the pass or
Bealach Chual a'scairt which leads across the Trotternish
Ridge to the village of Uig. In the early 20th century, a young
man from *Bhaltos* walked across the ridge by this pass to visit
a young lady in the township of Earlish. He asked her to
marry him. She replied, "No but I'll marry your brother!"
One wonders what his feelings were as he trudged back
home. He gave his brother the information and the marriage
did indeed take place.

On this road up from Brogaig is the township of Sartle. Near
here is the famous well, *Tobar na Slainte,* the Well of Health
whose waters were renowned for healing all human ailments.
It apparently lost its powers when a local crofter brought his
horse to be cured of colic. The horse was healed but no further
miracles have been recorded.

Returning to the main road once again, we come to the
townships of *Brogaig, Glasphein and Digg.*

At *Brogaig,* there is the benefit of small, but well kept public conveniences which mark the half-way point on our trip around Trotternish. Lots of our guests also take the opportunity to photograph the red telephone kiosk. These are, of course, rapidly disappearing in the UK due to the prevalence of mobile phones. There is no shortage of collectors willing to purchase them and several have been shipped abroad.

Glas-Pheighinn means green penny-land and has its origin in the system of Norse land-management. Each unit of land was referred to as "ounce land" or land rented out to a tacksman for an ounce of silver. This unit could then be subdivided into 10 or 20 parts known as *peighinn* or penny-lands.

The derivation of the name Digg is less complex. It means the ditch and this particular ditch, *Dreann na Stiubhartaich,* is very obvious as we enter one of the loveliest crofting communities in Skye.

This township epitomises how the crofting system should work. Each crofter has a small area of in-bye land, used for cropping or grazing, plus a share in the common grazing or out-bye land. Cattle, sheep and poultry are the stock on a typical croft. Such small-farming is not sufficient to allow a family to survive and so the crofter and/or his wife will have further full-time work. As you will see from the roadside signs, bed and breakfast or self-catering accommodation are common areas in which crofters diversify. Several of the young lads are also employed in the North Sea Oil Industry or in the Merchant Navy. These occupations allow for crofts to be worked during leave periods. Sheep-gathering for shearing, dipping and dosing are still community events.

Diatomite again

Loch Cuithir near Lealt was not the only site for the extraction of diatomite. *An Amach,* below *Dun Mor* at Digg also had stocks of the mineral. It had an advantage over *Loch Cuithir* as it was closer to the road and so it was not necessary to install a rail line. Instead, an overhead pulley system was employed. Known as the Blondin line, after Charles Blondin who crossed Niagara Falls on a tightrope in 1859, the rope and pulley carried the material from the loch down to the sea. The system operated for five years or so before World War I but was not revived after the war as stocks of diatomite were exhausted. The overhead line carried the material across the crofts of Digg and also over the tops of some of the houses. In October 1908, a local crofter, Mr Donald Gillies, claimed that a passing bucket belonging to the British Diatomite Co. Ltd. had damaged the chimney of his house. The company would only admit that its workers had rested a ladder against the gable end of the house and one employee had stood on Mr Gillies' chimney to measure the minimum height between chimney and bucket. They estimated the clearance to have been six feet.

CHAPTER 9

Flodigarry

Loch Seunta (the Loch of Enchantment) is fed by seven springs and was popular with Victorian tourists. It became known as a *"clootie loch"* where prayer cloths were hung on the hazel trees around its margins. Invalids came to bathe in the waters and it was reckoned a crime to take a trout from the sacred pool. A small carpark and path have recently been constructed for visitors to take the short walk down to it, thus avoiding intrusion on the crofts and gardens at Dunans.

Close by is another, but much deeper loch. *Loch Leum nam Bradh* at Dunans got its name, the Loch of the Jumping Quernstones, as follows. Quernstones or millstones were very necessary in ancient times, as every township had either a watermill or hand-mills to grind the corn for meal or flour. When MacDonald of the Isles took up residence at Duntulm Castle, several MacDonald watermills were set up in the area. All corn was to be ground only at these mills and at a cost! In order to encourage obedience to this order, the local quernstones were confiscated and put in the deepest and safest place — the bottom of this loch. As the quernstones were rolled down the hill, they bounced, leading to the name, Loch of the Jumping Quernstones.

There is a sequel to this tale. Quernstones are in demand by museums these days and what better place to get them than this loch! I've heard that divers have gone in here to retrieve both large and small ones. You may notice, as you approach the loch, that some wag has altered the roadsign from "Thank you for driving carefully", by deftly removing the letter "r"!

A third loch, by the roadside, was the scene of the sad drowning of a little girl, missing from home. The tale is connected with the supposed ability of particular individuals to "see into the future" or "Second Sight".

Two men were returning from peatcutting on the hill and were walking in single-file. The man behind noticed a bright patch or light on the jacket of his companion and drew attention to it. The jacket was duly removed and examined but the owner could see nothing amiss. The incident was disturbing, however, as such portents were regarded as a warning of a death in the community. On arrival in the village they learned of the missing child and joined the search party. On finding the little girl, it was that particular jacket that was used to cover the corpse.

Notice the broken rock where the road-makers have cut through some drumlins. These mounds were left by the retreating ice from the last ice-age which carried the broken basalt from beneath the cliffs as the glacier travelled in an easterly direction. Three prominent spurs of rock remain, giving testimony to the hardness of dolerite in dykes and sills.

Flodigarry was reputed to be the best grazing land in Skye, due to the influence of the underlying limestone strata. The Skye bardess Mary MacPherson extolled its fertility in one of her poems.

The famous Flora MacDonald and her husband, Allan of Kingsburgh, lived in a cottage here for eight years when he was given a tack of this land from the May term of 1751 until Whitsun 1759, before succeeding his father as laird at Kingsburgh. Indeed, five of their seven children were born here at Flodigarry. The present hotel was not their home. It was built by one of Flora's descendants Major R L Macdonald. Parts of the building and the interior decoration bear witness to the many years he spent in the Middle East as a soldier. Flora and Allan's cottage can still be seen in the hotel grounds.

Flora's husband Allan kept twenty or thirty cattle on the lush grazings and also acted as a drover, buying up cattle from other

Skye farmers. In the autumn, highland drovers made their way south to the large trysts or markets of central Scotland. The most popular trysts were at Falkirk and Crieff. As they travelled, it was traditional for the drovers to purchase more and more cattle. On arrival at Falkirk, Allan was known as *Ailean na Mile Mart*, Allan of the thousand cattle. Indeed, it is believed that it was Allan's great-grandfather, *Domhnull MacIain 'ic Sheumais* who first began this trade, which was to become the principal source of Skye's wealth for a century. This man was a celebrated warrior and bard of clan Donald who became the first MacDonald laird of Kingsburgh. The droving tradition was the means of creating many of our present day main roads throughout Scotland. The cattle had to be walked for several weeks and, to minimise discomfort, only the best *bealachs* between the hills were chosen. Our modern roads tend to follow *The Drove Roads of Scotland*. Because of the rough conditions, the cattle were often shod with leather or iron shoes, just as we shoe horses. The hardy highland cattle, with their long horns and shaggy coats, were able to survive the long trek but inevitably lost considerable condition along the way. Most of these cattle were black as it was reckoned that, these were most hardy. The fashion for brown and blonde highland cattle was encouraged by the Victorians; so much so, that the genes for the black highlanders were almost lost. In recent years, black cattle have again become popular. It's interesting to note that the origin of the term *Black Market* may have originated from the shady deals connected with the sale of black highland cattle which may or may not have been stolen! Some also believe that the word *blackmail* came into the English language from the tradition of paying rent, to the feudal superior, in livestock at the Martinmas term. (As was said earlier *mall* means rent).

As Skye is an island and there were few large ferryboats available in the 18th century, the cattle were made to swim across the narrows at Kylerhea to reach Glenelg on the mainland. In groups of six or eight, the cows were tied horn to tail, behind a small row boat. Cattle are in fact good swimmers although they don't get much practice nowadays! In the Agricultural Survey of 1813, the numbers crossing this narrow stretch of water were reckoned to be between 5000 and 8000 per annum! These are much higher numbers than we might expect, but the MacLeod chief had cattle shipped to Dunvegan from Lewis and Harris and then walked through Skye. Traditional overnight resting places became popular along the drovers' routes such as Borve and Sligachan.

Dynamic landscape.

On the road here at Flodigarry we get an excellent experience of the consequences of the weathering of the soft sedimentary rock layers beneath the surface strata. From time to time, the road is liable to severe subsidence and the successive layers and patches of tarmacadam, used to maintain the roadway, bear witness to the process.

An elderly gentleman from the township, *Murchadh Mor*, could remember, as a young boy, planting potatoes on part of his croft which is now under the sea. The landscape is indeed dynamic and these processes are happening within lifetimes rather than geological time!

In late July and early August there is a wonderful display of *bell heather* in bloom on the slopes near the Flodigarry Hotel. The purple haze is in contrast to the bright yellow of the attractive *ragwort* flowers. *Ragwort* is poisonous for herbivores but sheep and cattle tend to avoid it. Horses, which we regard as more intelligent, do not realise the danger and eat it fresh or wilted falling victim to serious intestinal troubles and liver damage. It can kill them! *Ragwort*, found on pasture land, should be pulled out and disposed of!

Sron Bhiornal, literally *Biornal's* nose, is the cliff above on the left. From certain angles it looks like the prow of a longship. Traditionally, this is the burial place of a Norse princess, (*Nighean Righ Lochlainn*), who some say, was the daughter of

King *Haakon*, who fell ill on a voyage. As her life ebbed away she asked her father to bury her on the headland in sight of the fleet. The winds of Norway would bring her a breath of her homeland.

A Danish couple, on one of our tours were interested in being shown Princess *Biornal's* grave. They reminded me that Denmark and Norway were, at one time, part of the same country. There is indeed a slab, in the rock at the cliff top, which may well be a grave!

Between Flodigarry and Kilmaluag, at Greap, is a single very lonely house. At least the residents are unlikely to have the difficulties with neighbours which we hear so much about these days! I think this would be the ideal home for someone contemplating taking up bagpipe playing as a new hobby!

CHAPTER 10

Between Flodigarry and Kilmaluag

We were very fortunate during the month of June and the first two weeks of July 2006 as we often spotted a White-tailed Sea Eagle hunting in this area. On occasions there were two birds present, possibly mates. Sea Eagles prey mainly on sea birds and fish. They are well known for their ability to catch quite large fish from beneath the surface of the sea, or fresh water loch, in the same manner as that employed by the Osprey, but a larger proportion of their diet is reckoned to be gulls and particularly the Fulmar. We surmised that, on windy days, when the choppy sea surface would make it difficult to spot fish, the eagles were possibly taking young rabbits from the plentiful supply on a green knoll in the foreground. This hunting technique is more often the province of the Golden Eagle, of which there are many more pairs in Skye, but the tell-tale white tail without the black terminal band confirmed that these were indeed adult Sea Eagles. The local RSPB officer was not aware of a nest in the immediate area and wondered if they were semi-mature birds whose first nesting attempt at Glenhinnisdale had failed. These very large birds, the largest in Britain, and the fourth largest bird of prey in the World, have broader wings and are bulkier birds than their Golden cousin and will hunt over a huge area of territory. In 2007, eleven pairs nested on Skye. In the same year there were around thirty nesting Golden Eagles.

By the roadside and on the nearby hill are the remains of concrete emplacements left behind from the Royal Air Force's wartime activities. Although they had no aircraft in the area, the RAF were the WWII coast watchers hereabout.

From the viewpoint above *Bagh nan Gunnaichean* (Bay of the Guns), named because of the sound of the waves crashing against the sea cliffs, we often see the spectacular diving of gannets hunting for sand-eels. What wonderful eyesight they must have to spot their prey from such a height. These birds nest on some of the distant islands, the largest colony being on the St. Kilda group, far to the west.

On a clear day the views from here are indeed wonderful, north, past Eilean Trodday (another St. Columba chapel here!) to the Island of Lewis, largest of the Western Isles, and the hills of the Island of Harris beyond the twin headlands of *Rubha Hunish* and *Rubha na h-Aiseig* which compose Skye's most northerly limit. To the east we can see the mountains of Sutherland. Sometimes visibility is upwards of thirty miles, coming as a surprise to city dwellers among our guests.

Kilmaluag

Kilmaluag was named for the cell or chapel of St. Moluag, Bishop of Lismore and a colleague of St. Columba, the ruins of which were recently traced nearby.

This monk is also associated with a church on Raasay, as well as the *Teampaill Moluaidh* at Ness in the Isle of Lewis.

On the right hand side of the road we see the typical shape of what was the local Kilmaluag school up until the mid 1960s. The teacher's house is at one end and the single classroom at right angles to it. As we pass, we notice that the schoolroom windows are high up so that the children would not be able to see out and be distracted from their lessons by the activities on the local crofts. These traditional school buildings were originally heated by peat-fired stoves. Each child was required to bring a peat to school from home each day to help keep the classroom warm.

It is interesting to note that Skye's first ever school was here at Kilmaluag, or rather, the neighbouring township of Shulista, in 1651. Sponsored by the Chief, Sir James Mac-

Donald for the benefit of his own family and professional servants, it was one of only four such schools in the Highlands at the time. Eighty students of various ages were able to attend in winter and about half that number in the summer due to their fishing and farming commitments. English, Gaelic, Latin and Greek were taught as well as Arithmetic and Navigation. Navigation would be important, as all commercial activity would then be by boat around the coast. Tracks and roads would have been of poor quality. The classical languages were of particular importance to the MacLean family of Shulista as this was their hereditary home. They occupied this township, rent free from the Lord of the Isles in return for their services as physicians to the MacDonalds of Duntulm. Son followed father in the profession, studying at Edinburgh University which of course continues to have an illustious Medical Faculty.

The important chiefs in the Highlands were known for their encouragement of the arts and traditional skills which became associated with particular families. We have mentioned the Beaton or Bethune family as skilled herbalists, able to distil concoctions and produce effective medicines from lots of plant materials, as well as dyes for tartan and tweed. They were sponsored by the Lords of the Isles and became valued members of court. The MacArthur family were the skilled hereditary pipers and composers of bagpipe music to Clan Donald at Duntulm Castle. They had their instruction at the Piping College at *Peingown* and practised their tunes on *Cnoc Phail*. The MacCrimmon family performed a similar service for the MacLeods of Dunvegan.

Harpists and fiddlers, able to tune into the mood of the moment were very welcome in the castles of the clans, as were singers and bards. These chiefs regarded themselves as monarchs and gathered skilled people around them.

Throughout the month of September the aftermath of the silage cut attracts greylag geese to the fields at Solitote. Occasionally, there are also some white-fronts grazing the crofts.

These birds are passage migrants on their way south from Iceland and Greenland for the winter. They are often to be seen on some of the small freshwater lochs. Loch Mealt seems to be popular with them. In spring, the process is repeated as they fly back north to breed.

CHAPTER 11

Duntulm Castle

Originally a Pictish fort, *Dun Dhaibhidh* (David's Fort), was later seized by the Vikings. When they were driven out by the Lords of the Isles in 1265 its fortifications were improved, (it has 50ft cliffs on three sides), and it became a castle. As the MacLeods and MacDonalds fought for supremacy in Skye, the castle changed hands several times. In the 16th Century, following the Battle of Trotternish, the MacDonalds again took possession under their Chief Donald Gorm. Thus began the heyday of Duntulm. It was Donald Gorm's proud boast that he had brought the earth of seven kingdoms to lay out his vegetable, fruit and flower gardens. In 1540, King James V of Scotland sailed into Score Bay on his Highland voyage to curb the power of the clans. He was much impressed and surprised by the strength, size and beauty of the Duntulm Castle and its grounds. Its position dominated the Minch, as any vessels seen to enter the waters between Skye and the Western Isles could be quickly intercepted by the war galleys of The Lord of the Isles.

The meaning of the name "Minch" seems to be the same as the term used by the French for the English Channel, "La Manche" – a sleeve. A narrow 'sleeve' of water between two landmasses.

On the rocks below the castle can be seen the deep grooves in the rocks worn by the keels of the war galleys and merchant ships. At one time the only entrance was by sea-gate with a strongly defended stairway up the cliff to the castle.

In the 16th Century handfasting or trial marriage was practised by the important clan leaders. Donald Gorm, for once at peace with the MacLeods of Dunvegan, took Margaret, the MacLeod Chief's sister, for a year's trial. He, however, took a dislike to Margaret and treated her with contempt. She had injured an eye and so Donald Gorm returned the damaged goods to MacLeod on a one-eyed horse led by a one-eyed servant with a one-eyed dog. This incident led to a fresh outburst of clan warfare (*Cogadh na Cailliche Caime*), the War of the One-eyed Woman which finally resulted in the bloody battle of *Corrie na Creich* in the heart of the Cuillins.

Donald Gorm was succeeded by Donald Gormson who was followed by Donald Gorm Mor. He was a powerful chief and he dispensed justice as he saw fit. There are three knolls in the vicinity of the Castle. *Cnoc a Cheartais*, the knoll of justice, *Ru Meanish*, the headland of pleas and *Cnoc a Croiche*, the hanging knoll. Another hill *Cnoc Rola* was used for a very nasty torture. The criminal was put in a barrel through which spikes were driven. The barrel was then rolled down the hill. The resulting wounds would be severe. If the victim died, the chief was satisfied that justice had been done. If he lived, there was a suspicion that witchcraft was involved. The gallows on the hangman's hill was a permanent fixture to instil awe into clansmen as well as foes.

Donald Gorm Mor had trouble from his enemies throughout his reign, but a constant thorn in his flesh was his cousin Hugh MacDonald, *Uisdean MacGillespic Cleirich*, who more than once plotted to murder the chief and plunge the clan back into unwanted wars. Hugh, normally resident in the Island of North Uist, built himself a castle at *Cudreach* near Uig, *Caisteal Uistean*, which had no windows in the walls. Entry was by a door in the roof which was reached by retractable ladders. Hugh wrote impertinently to Donald Gorm Mor inviting him to the house-warming. He also wrote to a certain William Martin of Marishadder with detail on how he should take this opportunity to murder the chief. The letters were sealed but were inadvertently mixed up. The intended victim got the murder plans. Hugh was apprehended after he had fled to a remote stronghold in a loch in Uist. He was discovered, dressed as a servant woman, grinding corn. His large size, however, gave him away. He was imprisoned in the dungeon of Duntulm Castle, fed salt beef and fish without drinking water. When his body was finally removed it was discovered that, in his agony of thirst, he had bitten deeply into the pewter cup in his desperation to get liquid. Hugh's bones were removed and kept in the window of the Kilmuir church for many years as a warning to others who might dare to rise up against the Chief of Clan Donald.

Although he had had three wives, Donald Gorm Mor had no son and so he was succeeded by his nephew, Donald Gorm Og.

After the rebellion of 1715, the MacDonald Duntulm lands were declared forfeit by the Crown as the next chief, *Domhnall a' Chogaidh* (Donald of the Wars), had supported the losing side. On the eve of the rising he had hosted a ball in the 'great hall' of Duntulm Castle in support of the Jacobite cause.

It is related that the MacDonald Clan abandoned Duntulm Castle as a result of a very sad accident. The chief's young heir, as a baby, was being held by his nurse at a window in the castle to watch the arrival of his father's war galley. He slipped out of the nurse's hands and was killed on the rocks beneath. The chief was devastated and insisted on moving his family to the unfortified, and much more modest, Monkstadt House. This occurred round about the year 1730. Much of the stone from Duntulm was used to build Monkstadt, thus accounting for the present state of the once proud stronghold. The punishment for the nurse was harsh. She was floated out to sea in a boat full of holes.

This far north part of Skye was probably where the Norsemen first settled. Names which end in –sta come from the Norse word '*stadhr*', meaning homestead. *Connista* and *Shulista* are examples. Names like these are particularly common in the Western Isles and this fits the known pattern of Norse settlement, beginning in the north and west and gradually moving to more southern parts. The Norse '*setr*' meaning sheiling or summer house equates to the word-ending -shader e.g. *Uigshader*. These names seem to be common towards the south of Loch Snizort, perhaps indicating the way in which the settlement began to spread out. These interesting ideas have been put forward by Alan Small of Dundee University.

The Islands off Rhu Hunish *(Flodaidh and Fladda Chuinn)*
Fladda Chuinn was held by the original Celtic inhabitants of Skye to be the *Tir Nan Og*, the Land of Eternal Youth. Here there is another St. Columba Chapel. The single, black altar stone is known as the weeping stone as it always appears wet. It has been suggested that the stone is, in fact, an example of a substance called obsidian, but where it came from is unknown.

Fishermen used to go ashore to pour a libation on the stone to implore for favourable weather and a good fishing. This intertwining of Christianity and ancient beliefs persisted in the islands down through the centuries.

Around Score Bay, the rockfalls remind us of the dynamic landscape of Trotternish. The enormous rocks are a discouragement for those planning to park caravanettes overnight in the lovely picnic areas with panoramic views of the Western Isles.

This is the best place to spot basking sharks. If you notice a pair of black fins in the water, it's likely to be the dorsal and tail fins of a single basking shark. These sharks live on plankton and krill and, although they can grow to an enormous size, are not aggressive. Some adventurous types aspire to swim with them but, as the sharks have a permanently open mouth, they may be in danger of being inadvertently scooped up.

Occasionally, leaping porpoises and bottle-nosed dolphins are spotted here in the bay.

CHAPTER 12

Clearances from Score Bay

It is important to keep some perspective on the notorious Highland Clearances. Undoubtedly, the land or indeed the sea round Skye, was not able to sustain the large population during the 18th century. Economic circumstances were such that many people felt themselves forced to seek a better life elsewhere. The clan chiefs, who, in the past, had been regarded as the benevolent fathers of the *clan* (or family), now saw themselves as landowners and aristocrats. They subdivided their sizeable estates and let them out to relatives and friends. These tenants were called tacksmen and the piece of land was a tack. In order to pay the rent to the chief, these tacksmen would sub-let smaller portions of the land to the common people while they farmed the best land themselves. Often one of the sub-let conditions was that a certain number of days' labour was required on the tacksman's farm. Inevitably, these days were demanded when it suited the feudal superior and not the sub-tenant. Further more onerous conditions were imposed when it suited, and failure to meet them resulted in dismissal from house and home. The substantial demand for plots of land and homes put the superiors in an increasingly strong position.

With improving communications, the chiefs began to spend more time in the cities of the south and to have their children educated there. Mixing with their rich friends meant that they required to "keep up with the Jones". They demanded higher rents from their tacksmen, who in turn raised the rents of the sub-tenants. One way for the chiefs to raise finance was by exploiting the wealth of seaware around the coasts. The kelp industry developed. Alginates for soap and glass-making were extracted from a sea weed called kelp by drying and then burning it in kilns fired by peat. Enormous quantities of kelp were required to make a little product and the industry was highly labour intensive (twenty tons of seaweed for one ton of ash). The people were offered small areas of poor quality land, a share in common grazing and a very small wage if they were willing to gather seaweed. The whole family would help in the work.

While prices for the ash remained high, the feudal superiors encouraged and cajoled more and more families to move to the rocky coast. When cheap barilla began to be imported from Spain after the Napoleonic Wars, the bottom fell out of the kelp market. The common people became destitute! They could not pay their rents and were threatened with eviction. Some sought work in the cities, while others sailed to Canada and Australia. Some landlords were prepared to give assisted passage, as the people, who had, in the past, been so important to the chiefs as soldiers and labourers, were now a burden. The MacDonalds purchased 100,000 acres of land in the Carolinas which they let to tacksmen and tenants. The price of sheep's wool in Britain was high so the landlords did not lose out! Pressure came on the tacksmen and sub-tenants, as lowland farmers were able to offer better terms for the grazing land. These new tenants brought in the *Caoraich Mhor*, the big sheep, or cheviot sheep (as opposed to the smaller native black-faced sheep of the islands). The Lowland surnames of Stoddart, Lockhart, Robertson, Brown and Bruce became common in Skye as the new tenants and their shepherds moved in. The local sub-tenants, now called crofters, were displaced as they had no security of tenure. Any who were not prepared to leave their place of birth were forced into overcrowded townships on the poorest land along the sea coast to survive on shellfish, or on fishing if they were lucky. As many had no land at all, they were termed cottars. The area around Score Bay was one such place.

Having lost their lands at Duntulm by Crown confiscation after 'the 1715', the MacDonalds bought them back in 1723 for the huge sum of £23,000 which no doubt, caused them to be very careful who to support in 1745!

In 1847, Lord MacDonald, now based at Armadale in Sleat, finally sold up to Captain William Fraser of Culbokie for the sum of £85,000.

Captain Fraser set up his residence at Uig where he built a large mansion. The crofters were cleared off the best lands to make the sheep farms of Monkstadt, Duntulm and Scudda-burgh. A factor or estate manager, William Malcolm, was appointed and he decided to increase the rent for those crofters who were still in possession of an acre or two. An increase of 30% on rents, that they already had difficulty in paying, was the final straw for many.

Some felt forced to leave, others were forcibly evicted for amassing rent arrears, while only a few were prepared to make a stand.

Following unrest in other parts of Skye, the Sheriff for the County of Inverness, William Ivory, arranged for a contingent of Royal Marines and mainland Police Officers to come to the island in order to deal with the offenders. Having been frustrated by the crofters of Braes, he did not use half measures here. The gunboats 'Jackal' and 'Seahorse' supported his Sheriff Officers and anchored at Kilmaluag. They marched on Bornasketaig and Herbusta to issue summonses and eviction notices. Undeterred, the crofters' women folk linked arms and defied the efforts of the authorities to serve the legal warrants on their men, at the same time making clear that their fight was with the landlord and not the crown by flying a Union Flag. Although arrests and imprisonment followed, national publicity helped the cause of The Land League.

CHAPTER 13

Museum of Island Life

The main house in this superb museum was once the home of Katie Anne MacMillan who was born here in the early years of the 20th century and is now resident in Portree.

The Museum shows what life in this area was like at the beginning of the 1900s and, for its modest charge, is well worth a visit. Our tour always stops here for 20 minutes or so and all our guests have been most impressed. A number, who have their own transport, opt to return for a longer visit on another occasion during their holiday. Opened in 1965, it is lovingly and knowledgably run by local historian Jonathan MacDonald and his family. In the complex of thatched cottages one can view many historical documents and photographs as well as domestic and crofting implements.

The original blackhouses were so named from the smoke of the peat fires which pervaded them. When the fire was in the middle of the floor, and there was no provision for the smoke to escape via a chimney, the houses were very dim and black, both inside and out.

Many of our visitors enquire why most Skye people nowadays paint their houses white. I wonder if this is a reaction to the dark and gloomy blackhouses in which our, not so distant, ancestors were forced to exist?

From here the views to the Western Isles are breathtaking. We see the Outer Hebrides in an arc from Uist in the south to the Shiant Isles and the Isle of Lewis.

The cottages of the museum require regular upkeep, not an easy task these days, as the absence of skilled thatchers presents a problem.

Kilmuir Cemetery

This much visited local graveyard is still in use but has four gravestones which are of particular interest historically.

The most famous, and the main reason for the high visitor numbers, is that of the heroine Flora MacDonald who rescued Prince Charles Edward Stewart and sailed him **over the sea to Skye.**

Flora was born in Milton, South Uist in 1722 and died in Skye in 1790. We will tell more of her very adventurous life in the next few pages.

> *"Her name will be mentioned in history and if courage and fidelity be virtues, mentioned with honour."*

Dr. Samuel Johnston

One of the famous MacArthur pipers is buried here and his unfinished gravestone is interesting.

> *HERE LYES*
> *THE REMAINS OF*
> *CHARLES MAC*
> *KARTER WHOSE*
> *FAME AS AN HON*
> *EST MAN AND*
> *REMARKABLE PIP*
> *ER WILL SURVIVE*
> *THIS GENERATION*
> *FOR HIS MANNERS*
> *WERE EASY & RE*
> *GULAR AS HIS*
> *MUSIC AND THE*
> *THE MELODY OF*
> *HIS FINGERS WILL*

The story goes that the stone mason, realising that he would not be paid, due to the sudden death of MacArthur's son, who was to foot the bill, stopped work immediately! An alternative reason may well be that the mason may have realised that he had chiselled the word "the" twice, at lines 13 and 14, and so abandoned the carving to begin again!! No word processors with a delete button in those days!

A "stolen" knight effigy from the tomb of one of the Scottish kings on Iona marks the grave of *Aonghas na Gaoithe* or Angus of the Wind, a pirate of the Martin clan. He got his name from his wandering nature and determination to go to sea in all weathers. Angus is supposed to have carried this gravestone up from the beach on his back! A likely story, as it would take at least six men to lift it! He is reputed to have married a Danish Princess Bernice and had seven sons.

The fourth interesting grave is that of the last of the MacLean doctors of Shulista. John MacLean died in 1793 aged 85. He was highly commended by Dr. Johnston for his intellect and understanding of current affairs. As you might expect, the carving on his tombstone is in Latin with which he was very familiar, having learned it at the little school at Shulista.

It is interesting to note the profuse growth of the lichen known as *Old Man's Beard* on many of the gravestones in the cemetery. No lichen grows on the sides exposed to the prevailing wind!

Seton Gordon CBE

By the roadside is another very interesting memorial to a remarkable man who made his home here at Upper Duntulm.

During his 46 years living at Duntulm he wrote 27 books. It's said that his main reason for coming to live here was that he would be able to see golden eagles on a daily basis. Behind his home, and visible from the rear windows of Upper Duntulm House, is *Creag Sneosdal* where eagles have nested for centuries.

This Gaelic verse indicates their presence in the distant past;

Creag Sniosadal nam Biatach,
'far an do bhog Fionn a chas ann
Dh'fhag e 'n t-uisge donn.

Creag Sneasdal of the eagles,
in whose loch, Fingal dipped his foot,
leaving the water brown.

Seton's knowledge of the birds of Skye, the Highlands and of Northern Europe was unsurpassed. I was fortunate to meet him in 1968 when, as a schoolboy, he helped me to write an article on "The Birds of Skye" for the magazine '*Skye '68*'. Born in 1886, he died in 1977. How pleased he would have been with the success of the project to reintroduce the white-tailed eagle to Scotland and that so many pairs are now nesting in Skye!

Continue around the narrow township road through Peingown, the ancestral home of the MacArthur pipers, and by the crofting township of Herbusta. The main reason I suggest this detour is the possibility of seeing the elusive Golden Eagles. On a number of occasions during the summers of 2006 and 2007 we were fortunate, as they made hunting sorties over *Beinn a Sca*.

This quiet road is also ideal for spotting some of our summer visiting birds. The white flash on the rear of the little birds which flit away from the front of the vehicle indicates the presence of wheatears and the dark capped birds calling from the top of fence posts are stonechats. Their call sounds exactly like two pebbles being knocked together. Round the houses and barns of Herbusta, the young swallows circle and twist as they perfect their fly-catching skills. In spring, the west-facing slope of the hill is covered in beautiful clumps of primroses. In May, these are replaced by bluebells before the arrival of the ubiquitous bracken.

CHAPTER 14

The Herring Fishing

At the beginning of the 20th century there was a boom in the herring fishing industry which was a God-send to the poor people of these islands. Score bay was one of the many places where the herring shoaled in their millions. Boats came from all around the area to catch the 'silver darlings'. There was work for the fishermen but also for their women-folk whose duties were to pack the salted herring in barrels. A very important export trade developed with the countries of northern Europe. Fishermen and the Herring Girls followed the shoals as they moved round the north and down the east coasts of Scotland, as far south as Yarmouth and Lowestoft in England. Not only were the salted herring important, but fresh herring was sent by rail to the cities of the south where they proved a valuable protein source, particularly for the urban poor.

Other work was in short supply and the purchase of Kilmuir Estate by the Congested Districts Board in 1904 was welcomed, as its ideas had proved effective elsewhere. In 1908 a basket-making project was started in Kilmuir. Baskets were to be used for the transport of fresh herring. The present Village Hall in Kilmuir is more commonly called "The Factory" by local people. It was here that basket-weaving was begun. The street of houses opposite has been named Willows Road, as local growing of the osiers, to be used in the weaving, was encouraged. Shopping baskets, log baskets, chairs, tables and cradles were also produced. In 1910 a larger factory was built and, on the death of Dr. Barbour, the instigator of the development, Highland Home Industries of Edinburgh took over the project, adding weaving and rug making to the skills of local people. Eventually production ended in 1956 due to market recession and the "Factory" was gifted to the community.

The Kilvaxter Souterrain

In 1992, along with a group from Portree High School and accompanied by Hector MacKenzie from *Hungladder*, we visited a souterrain at *Lachasay*, near *Herbusta*. Little did we know that within ten years another underground chamber would be discovered, excavated and made available as a visitor attraction in this area. Thirtyone of these iron-age chambers have so far been discovered in Skye, but this one is the largest and most convenient to visit as it is by the roadside at *Kilvaxter*.

Phil James one day discovered a small hole in his field. On inspection this proved to be a collapsed roof stone of the structure which lay beneath the modern field level. Roger Miket of the Highland Council Museum service and a team of helpers began to excavate the site in a strict scientific manner. The 2000 year old structure had remained in excellent condition, in spite of horse and tractor ploughs being used in the field over the years. These structures were probably built by the Pictish people to protect their grain stores from winter weather and enemy raiders. They may also have served as protection for the human population themselves although the passages are narrow and confined. During the excavation, there were some interesting finds including a fine wine glass and a small horde of English thirteenth century coins of the reign of Henry II.

CHAPTER 15

The Flora Macdonald story.

This is the most romantic of all the historical stories connected with the Isle of Skye.

> *"Speed bonnie boat like a bird on the wing*
> *"Onward" the sailors cry;*
> *Carry the lad that is born to be king,*
> *Over the sea to Skye."*

The lad was Prince Charles Edward Louis Phillipe Casimir Stuart and considered, by the Jacobites, the followers of his grandfather the exiled King James II, to be the heir to the thrones of England, Scotland and Ireland.

James had died in 1701 and his son, Charles' father "the Old Pretender", had had three unsuccessful attempts to regain the crown. He now regarded this as an impossible task. Charles, however, at 24 years of age was full of youthful vigour and, with the aid of Louis XV of France, who was the avowed enemy of the English, was confident that he could win back the British throne for the Stuarts. Charles was therefore called "the Young Pretender".

As fate would have it, just before the ships and troops left France, a mighty gale blew up destroying the boats and cargo destined for the English shores. Louis was keen to postpone the planned action, but the headstrong Charles had made up his mind to go and would not be persuaded otherwise. "Conquer or Die" was his motto. He sold his jewels and bought two ships, the 'Elizabeth' and the 'Du Teilly'. Not long at sea, the ships were intercepted by the English warship 'Lion' and the 'Elizabeth' was forced to return to France. Charles sailed on with a few followers in the 'Du Teilly', landing on the Island of Eriskay. The Clan Chiefs were cautious. Many had lost their lands after the failed rebellions in 1715 and 1719. Landing on the Scottish mainland at Arisaig, Charles got the support of Cameron of Locheil, but MacDonald, Lord of the Isles, sided with the Hanovarians and MacLeod of Dunvegan sat on the fence. MacLeod of Raasay, MacDonald of Keppoch and MacKinnon of Strath, however, were loyal to Charles and on the 19th August 1745 the standard was raised at Glenfinnan. They marched south and took the city of Edinburgh with hardly a fight. The Prince and his men created revelry in Holyrood Palace. The white cockade was proudly on display. Outside Edinburgh, at Prestonpans, the Hanoverian garrison offered some resistance but the sight of 5000 Highlanders weakened the heart of their commander, General John Cope. A short battle took place and the wild Highland charge was sufficient to achieve victory. Johnny Cope fled. So far so good, now it was on to London. The snowy wintry weather, lack of food, news that King George and the Hanovarians were mustering thousands of troops and arguments among Charles' advisers forced the army to turn around at Derby. Little did they know that London was in a panic. There had been a run on the Bank of England and there was only a ragged army on Finchley Common to defend the capital. Had they pushed on, things could well have been different.

The retreat north began, culminating in defeat at the battle of Culloden Moor on 16th April 1746.

Following the defeat, the Duke of Cumberland, leader of the victorious Hanovarians, ordered his troops to go around the battlefield killing the wounded and prisoners in cold blood. He is well-named *The Butcher Cumberland*. The Prince, however, escaped with a few followers via Loch Arkaig and Loch Morar to Borrodale where he learned of the price of £30,000 on his head. One of his oldest followers, Donald MacLeod of Galtrigill in Glendale, came to his aid and ferried him across to the Island of Benbecula. From here Charles went to Harris, Lewis and the Uists, moving secretly and stealthily as he sought a French ship to return him to the continent but, though he was seen by many, his whereabouts was not revealed in spite of the huge incentive. The islands were occupied by a very large contingent of redcoats and it was only a matter of time before the Prince would be captured. Meanwhile, Flora MacDonald was visiting her brother in Milton, South Uist. Flora was the daughter of the late Ranald MacDonald of Milton and was thus a descendant of the Chiefs of Clan Ranald. On her mother's side she was a descendant of the Chiefs of Sleat. Flora's mother was re-married to Hugh MacDonald of Armadale who was currently in charge of a company of the Hanoverian army in the Western Isles. A plan was conceived to spirit the Prince back to Skye. Hugh MacDonald provided his step-daughter with a letter and passports giving permission for her to go to Armadale Castle to her mother, accompanied by her Irish maid Betty Burke. Betty Burke was none other than the Prince in disguise.

Sailing from Roisinish in Benbecula on Saturday 28th June the small boat set out for Skye, avoiding the government vessels which were patrolling the Minch.

As they were sailing by the headland of Waternish Point they spotted a band of militia men who hailed them to land. The crew pulled hard on the oars to get away and promptly the militia fired at them. Luckily they escaped and were able to land at *Allt a'Chuain* in the Bay of Kilbride, (now called Prince Charles' Point). This was close to the House of Monkstadt, headquarters of the MacDonalds. Flora made for the house leaving "Betty Burke" and the others by the boat. Here she met with Lady Margaret MacDonald. The reason for her visit was understood by her cousin Lady Margaret, but there was need for secrecy as Lieutenant Alexander MacLeod of Talisker, in charge of the local militia searching for the Prince, was billeted in the house. Since Flora had come from Uist, she was questioned, during the Sunday lunch, by the officer about rumours of the Prince's whereabouts on the islands. Flora answered with calmness and composure, dispelling any possible suspicion that she might know anything of Charles' whereabouts. In later days "she often laughed in good humour with this gentleman, on her having so well deceived him". Also present at the meal was Alexander MacDonald of Kingsburgh, factor to Sir Alexander MacDonald of Monkstadt. He, Flora and Lady Margaret planned the next move. The Prince would go to the factor's home at Kingsburgh, 14 miles away. They set off in the still of the evening on foot. Flora and two companions followed on horseback, arriving at Kingsburgh shortly after the walkers. Mrs MacDonald rose from her bed to prepare a meal for the fugitives. Not surprisingly, it was towards dawn before the party retired to their beds. The Prince slept till late afternoon on the Monday. Meanwhile, Flora and the Prince's companion, Neil MacEachain, set out for Portree to make further plans for the escape. In the evening, the Prince and the factor set off, after giving Mrs MacDonald a lock of his hair as a thank you for her kindness. (She also kept the Skye Linen sheets from the bed on which the Prince slept, "unwashed", so that she and Flora would be buried in one each). This illustrates the reverence they felt for the Prince.

Flora, Neil and Charles MacNab the Innkeeper made arrangements with Captain Roy MacDonald for taking Charles on the next stage of his journey. Roy MacDonald met Charles on the outskirts of Portree and brought him to MacNab's Inn (now the Royal Hotel) to meet up again with Flora. As they parted and Charles thanked her for all that she had done for him, he said; "For all that has happened, I hope, Madam, that we shall some day meet at St. James'."

"Fareweel to the lad I shall ne'er see again,
Fareweel to my hero, the gallant an' young."

That night the Prince was spirited across to Raasay but only remained there one night as Cumberland's troops had burned out a number of houses in retaliation for MacLeod of Raasay joining the rebellion. From here he landed back at Nicolson's rock in Portree harbour, spent the night in a disused byre, then set off south. He passed through Strath, eventually arriving at Kilmaree where Captain MacKinnon arranged for him to be taken to the mainland at Mallaig, then to Loch Morar where a French Ship lay at anchor awaiting him. Prince Charles lived a further 40 years in exile, but he never once communicated with Flora or those other loyal and devoted men and women who had bravely saved him from his enemies.

Flora was apprehended and, although always treated with kindness, was arrested and taken to Edinburgh and eventually to London. She was confined to the Tower of London for eight months. Here she met the Crown Prince Frederick, son of George II. He enquired of her why she had been so kind to the rebel. Her wise reply was that she would have done the same for him if he had been in similar circumstances. Prince Frederick now became her greatest fan and petitioned his father, the king, for her release. When her story was made public there was great excitement and sympathy for her. It was now 1747, fear of rebellion was now past, and an Act of Indemnity was brought in, whereby all prisoners from the '45, including Flora, were set free. She returned to Skye, being feted from town to town as she travelled north, and married Allan MacDonald of Kingsburgh. Her adventures were by no means over!!

In 1759, having lived at Flodigarry for eight years, Allan and Flora with their five children, moved to Kingsburgh with a view to Allan taking over from his father as the Factor of the MacDonald Estate. Cattle prices had fallen and farming was in recession. Two more children were born to them at Kingsburgh. Allan's mother had died so Flora was in charge of the household. However, Allan and his father fell out over the running of the estate. Allan took the tack of Kingsburgh but gave up the factorship. Allan and Flora lived there happily until his father's death in 1772.

In 1773 Dr Samuel Johnson and his friend Boswell visited them at Kingsburgh. Johnson described Allan as: *"....completely the figure of a gallant Highlander"* and Flora as: *"a name that will be mentioned in history and if courage and fidelity be virtues, mentioned with honour"*.

Johnston slept in the very bed that the Prince had occupied 29 years earlier. When he left in the morning, they found a scrap of paper on the bedside table with the Latin words: *"Quantum cedat virtutibus aurum"* – *"with virtue weighed what worthless trash is gold"*.

Next year, given the poor economic situation in Skye, Allan and Flora with sons Alexander, 18 and James, 16, left for North Carolina to secure a tract of land in the new world. The rest of the family were cared for by relatives, as their parents planned to return for them when all was settled. Before too long, however, the troubles in the colonies broke out into the American War of Independence. Allan served with the Loyalist Army in the Royal Highland Emigrant Regiment, as did their two sons. Flora was now alone and having to defend their new homestead. The house was plundered before her eyes and she was robbed of all her possessions and had an arm broken. Allan and the boys were all captured, following the Battle of Moore's Creek in 1776, and were prisoners of war until, in 1779, when he was able to return to his regiment and to arrange for Flora to sail for home in Scotland. At the end of the Independence War Allan joined her and they eventually settled with a small piece of land at Peinduin near Kingsburgh. In 1790 Flora passed away at their new home. Her funeral at Kilmuir was one of the largest ever seen in Skye with at least three thousand in attendance, a testimony to her fame and popularity. Two years later Allan died and was buried beside his wife.

CHAPTER 16

The Headland of Bornaskitaig

The MacLeod and MacDonald chiefs had agreed a galley race from Rodel in the Isle of Harris to determine who would rule Trotternish. The galleys were approaching this point of land and the MacLeod chief was in the lead. The rules stated that the first hand to touch land could claim it for their own. The MacDonald chief rose up in his galley, cut of his right hand at the wrist with a blow of his *sgian dubh* and threw his hand to shore, thus claiming victory.

To this day, the crest of Clan Donald has the symbol of a severed right hand and the Latin *"Per Mare per Terras"*, by sea and by land. This same motto is also, very appropriately, claimed by the Royal Marines.

Uamh an Oir

On the sea shore by Bornaskitaig is *Uamh an Oir*, the Cave of Gold into which a MacArthur piper marched to encounter a sea-monster that was ravaging the crops of Trotternish. The refrain of his tune was to the effect that calves would be full grown cows and boys would be men ere ever he returned.

Monkstadt

The arable land in Kilmuir was always of high quality.

"To reap in Monkstadt" became a proverb across the High-lands and this area was called *"The Granary of Skye——Laughing with corn"*.

The sloping fields facing west were dominated by a large body of freshwater, *Loch Chaluim Chille*, St. Columba's Loch. The loch was so named, because *Eilean a Loch*, in its waters, was the site of an ancient monastery described by one authority as the best example of a monastic establishment in Britain. Outlines of the original beehive buildings are still clearly visible. Several attempts were made to drain the waters during the 17th century, as it was recognised that the exposed land would be particularly fertile. Following a survey by Dr. MacLeod, the *Dotair Ban* in 1819, the drains were broadened and cleared towards the sea. The project took six years and involved a great deal of work by the local people who were allocated shares in the "loch". Predictions proved accurate and the quality of the oats and bere barley that this soil produced was said to be second to none. No sooner was the land reclaimed from the water than the proprietor of Monkstadt Farm "reclaimed" it for his own use. Owing to the intense labour required to keep the mile of drains clear of rushes and reeds, the ground has gradually reverted to swamp, unsuitable for heavy machinery. Another crop which proved successful here in the early days was flax, from which developed a linen industry. Skye Linen sheets were regarded as a sign of status in Highland hotels of the 19th century. The local township name *Linicro* literally means linen crop. There are several other placenames in Skye connected with the trade, three *Lyndales*, one each in Snizort, Duirinish and Bracadale, as well as *Lynton* in Staffin.

Has climate change been at work in Skye? In the 1950s I recall substantial fields of oats and late-cut hay. Our summers, in recent years, have tended to be too wet for such harvests, while our winters have been warm, wet and free of frost and snow. Our position in the northwest has, of course, brought us the benefits of the Gulf Stream but our weather has undergone a gradual change during my lifetime. Whether this has been caused by Global Warming, due to human activity or for other reasons, we must leave for the 'experts' to judge.

Monkstadt House became the MacDonald stronghold after they left Duntulm Castle. It was here that Prince Charlie, dressed as Betty Burke her Irish Servant, was taken by Flora MacDonald after the escape from Uist.

On the shore near Monkstadt is Prince Charles' Point, where he and Flora Macdonald made landfall, although it proved unsafe for him to visit the house.

Nowadays there are two delightful thatched cottages for weekly rent at either end of the Totescore township. Unlike the blackhouses of the past, these have all the modern conveniences one might wish for.

CHAPTER 17

Uig

The name *Uig* or *Vik* is a Norse one meaning sheltered bay. The name is common around the north and west of Scotland and the islands. Prestwick in Ayrshire, Wick in Caithness and Lerwick in the Shetland Isles are examples, as well as names ending in –aig e.g. Mallaig, Camustianavaig and Fiscavaig.

The Viking fleet would have made use of these harbours on their raiding and, later, trading excursions. Nowadays, Uig is the port from which twice daily sailings of the 'M V Hebridean Isles' depart for Lochmaddy in North Uist and Tarbert in Harris. Caledonian MacBrayne operate a very efficient roll-on, roll-off system, and the ship disembarks and embarks upwards of 100 vehicles in its 25 minutes turnaround time at the pier.

The original pier, *King Edward's Pier,* was built in 1894 at a cost of £9000 but suffered severe damage in a violent storm, but not before King Edward himself had visited Uig in 1902.

This lovely little village is now home to The Isle of Skye Brewery which makes ales and stouts *Black Cuillin, Red Cuillin, Blaven and Hebridean Gold* in their premises by the pier. Uig Pottery is also a tourist magnet where one can view the skilled potters at work.

Another of the ubiquitous Martins is remembered in Uig.

The John Martin Hospital was built in Uig in the early 1900s to provide medical attention and hospital care for the sick poor in the communities of Trotternish. Later, it was taken into the NHS and was the Maternity unit for north Skye with over 100 births per year. The building is now used as the SYHA hostel and is very popular with our visitors as it is perched in a lovely spot overlooking the sea.

Around the hillsides that circle the bay, buzzards are a common sight. They seem to delight in soaring on the updraughts and the sea breezes.

Captain Fraser

As mentioned earlier, Captain William Fraser built himself a villa or lodge on the edge of the bay when he took over the MacDonald Estate lands in 1847. Neither he nor his factor, William Malcolm, were popular, as they pressurised and evicted crofters and cottars alike. On 13th October 1877, a freak flash-flood caused the banks of the Rivers Conon and Rha to combine, as more than seven inches of rain fell within a few hours. The old Uig cemetery was overwhelmed, coffins were exposed and washed towards the sea, and severe damage was done in the glens. The waters totally destroyed Captain Fraser's home. Many regarded this happening as a judgement from God for the proprietor's callous attitude towards his destitute tenants. "*The Highlander*", a newspaper which espoused the crofters' cause said;

"*The belief is common throughout the parish that the disaster is a judgement upon Captain Fraser's property.——as if the dead in their graves rose to perform the work of vengeance which the living had not the spirit to execute. The living do not hesitate to express their regret that the proprietor was not in the place of his manager when he was swept away.*"

Captain Fraser sued the newspaper for the insult but was only awarded £50 costs. This sum was sufficient however, to put "*The Highlander*" out of business.

The round tower at Uig is known as Captain Fraser's Folly, built for no other reason than to keep some of the local men in work and out of trouble, lest Fraser become the focus of their attention!

Sheader, Balnaknock (The Fairy Glen)

This is yet another example of the dynamic landscape of Trotternish. The hillocks have been formed by geological processes associated with the movement of ice at the conclusion of the last ice-age. There are drumlins and exposed stacks of hard basalt similar to those found at Flodigarry. The effect of these, combined with the hazel woodland and little loch, is to evoke a feeling of being in a child's story book.

A local legend claims that a fairy sits, in turn, each night of the year, on the 365 knolls. What she does on leap years is not related!

Corncrakes

When I was young, corncrakes were common here in the fields below Rankin the Baker's shop. Since then, these shy birds, which were heard but rarely seen, have forsaken the mainland of Scotland and their numbers have been severely reduced in the islands. The RSPB, with the cooperation of the island crofters, has endeavoured to encourage their return. Rather than cutting grass for silage in the early summer, the crop is left longer until the fledglings have left their nests and are able to run around. When mowing begins, it is from the centre of the field outwards, so that the young birds can escape to the field margins for protection until they are old enough to fly.

On the hill above Uig are the remains of an ancient bronze age stone circle. The main centre-stone, Clach Ard Uig can be seen from the road. It had lain flat for many years but was re-erected in the early 1900s. It is said that, Kenneth MacKenzie, the Brahan Seer prophesied; *"Olaidh an fitheach a shath bharr an lair air mullach Clach-art Uig"*. The raven will drink its fill off the ground from the top of the High Stone of Uig. Presumably this is a reference to the fall of the stone from its original position.

As we drive between Uig and Earlish we have a fine view of *Ben Aketil* and its 10, 2.3-megawatt wind turbines. Erected in

2007, it is said that this windfarm is more than capable of producing sufficient green energy to satisfy all the electricity requirements of the island —- while the wind blows of course. The power is fed into the National Grid. This project, along with the Hydro scheme at Storr Lochs, makes Skye a net exporter of electricity to the rest of the nation.

I personally do not find the turbines visually intrusive and feel that, even if they were, it would be a small price to pay for reducing the effects of pollution and Global Warming associated with electricity production from fossil fuels. As it is, 400 local shareholders in The Isle of Skye Renewables Co-operative are set to benefit more directly.

Caisteal Uisdein (Hugh's Castle)

This castle, already mentioned, was an almost impregnable fortress with no windows or doors in the walls. Entry was by ladder through the thatched roof. To this day it is in a reasonable state of repair, unlike Duntulm Castle, but requires a trek across the fields of *Cuidrach* farm to visit it.

The lands of *Cuidrach*, (place of the forceful or determined ones), was given to *Donal MacIain ic Shamus* by the Lord of the Isles, as a reward for his prowess in battle.

CHAPTER 18

Kingsburgh

The name seems to show a connection with royalty, but this is not in fact the case as it is a mistranslation into English of the Gaelic name meaning tax town or toll town.

From ancient times the occupants of this township were authorised to levy taxes on all traffic moving up and down Loch Snizort. Although this is Skye's longest fjord, I have not seen any explanation of why ships might be expected to pay for the privilege of passing up and down the loch. Perhaps the answer lies in the fact that there was another St. Columba's Chapel at the head of Loch Snizort and that there was, at one time, considerable pilgrim traffic to and from what Dr. Alisdair Maclean has described as *The Cathedral of the Isles*.

It is interesting that the names of the rivers Hinnisdal and Romesdal, which we cross over on our way south, come from the Norse. There are two similar rivers, close to each other and with the same names in Norway!

Eyre Stones

At Eyre, by the seaside, there are two large standing stones. Local people tell me that there was originally a third which the giant *Caoilte* threw across the loch. It can now be seen at *Skerinish* point. The three stones had formed a tripod on which the *Feinne* or Fingalians perched their pot in order to cook venison stew. On one occasion, when deer had not been sighted for many days, a pot of shellfish was put on. This was regarded as a very much inferior dish, only to be consumed as a last resort. Suddenly, a cry was heard that the deer hunt had been successful and the giant hounds, led by *Luath* and *Brann*, had discovered a herd on *Creag nam Meann*. The pot of shellfish stew was knocked over and the contents splattered on the rocks nearby. They are now speckled and spotted and given the name *Creagan a' Bhalgaim* (rocks of the mouthful). *Fingal, Cuchullin* and their followers enjoyed the superior feast.

Cuchullin, the Irish hero of the *Ossianic* tales, served a seven year apprenticeship learning the art of warfare from *Sgathach*, Skye's female warrior. (Was she in fact a personification of the island?). He has given his name to the Cuillin mountains and *Fingal* had his seat on the hill behind Portree (*Suidh Fhinn*).

The Church of Scotland, Kensaleyre

This magnificent church building, designed by Gillesbuig Graham, has recently been renovated by a local building firm under the watchful eye of Historic Scotland. The aisle of the church had been paved with red flagstones quarried on the Island of Soay. During the renovation process 13,000 slates were replaced on the roof. The vestry of the church is on the first floor, with a door directly into the pulpit and above the stable for the minister's pony!

This was once the church of the well known preacher *Maighstir Ruaraidh*, Rev. Roderick MacLeod. He was one of only two Skye ministers of the Established Church to leave for the Free Church of Scotland at the Disruption of 1843. The other was Rev. John Glass of Bracadale. It is said that, through the preaching of those two, and lay-preachers like John Farquharson and the blind Donald Munro, most of the population of Skye was attracted to the Free Church, in spite of their ministers.

Perhaps another attraction was the fact that most ministers of the Established Church, but not all, failed to show sympathy, or to stand up for the people whose land and homes were being destroyed or confiscated. The ministers, through patronage, owed their appointments to the landowners, and tended to take the side of "the powers that be which are ordained of God", while encouraging the people to submit to their superiors and betters. The Rev. Roderick MacLeod was appointed moderator of the Free Church in 1863. In his moderatorial address, he referred to the outstanding contribution made by Skyemen to the British Army and Empire in the period before 1815.

"The men of Skye were of more value in those days. Times have changed. The cry is now, ' Away with them! Away with them!' Sheep, it appears, are more worthy of keeping."

Only after many years of open-air services, were the inhabitants of Trotternish eventually granted permission and land on which to build Free Churches. Dr. Sorley MacLean however comments that: "By the time of the crofter resurgence in the 1880s, the Free Church had, to a certain extent, become a church of the Establishment."

Skye's Contribution to the Military

In the light of Rev. Roderick's comments on the value of the men of Skye as soldiers, the numbers can be put into context from a statement made by Rev. Dr. Norman MacLeod known as *Caraid nan Gaidheal* (the Highlander's friend). *"The Island of Skye made a contribution to the fighting forces of the Crown during a period of forty years, from 1797, of, 21 lieutenant-generals and major-generals, 45 colonels, 600 commissioned officers, 10,000 common soldiers and 120 pipers."*

Dun Cruinn (the round fort) on the peninsula above Carn Liath was once another of the signalling duns. Nearly all of its stones have been pilfered for housing.

Carn Liath — the grey cairn (one of three in Trotternish)
This enormous mound of stones at the head of Kensaleyre (*Ceann Sal Eighre*) is believed to be a Neolithic burial chamber

or chambered cairn. A tale from Adamnan's *Life of St Columba* hints that it may be the burial place of *Artbranan*, leader of the Picts and the first Christian convert in Skye.

"*When the blessed man (St Columba) was staying in the Isle of Skye, he struck with his staff a spot of land in a certain place, near to the sea, and said to his companions: 'Strange to say my children, today on this spot of land a heathen old man will be baptised, will die and will be buried.'*

Apparently this happened as predicted and "*his companions heaped a large pile of stones and buried him.*"

Place-names all around this area seem to bear testimony to the presence of a very important church. The whole valley of the Snizort river, including Skirinish and Tote up to Peiness, is still referred to as *Ung na Cille*, the ounce land of the church. *Prabost* suggests the priest's dwelling, and Dr. MacLean speculates that *Tobhta* refers to the ancient ruins of the cathedral in the river, overlooked by Tote township.

St Columba Snizort Cemetery

St Columba's earliest visit to Skye is believed to have been in AD585. He died in 597AD. Although there are several ruined churches or monasteries in north Skye which are named after this saint, there is some evidence to suggest that this one was his principal abode while in the island. A large rock, one of the two *Clachan Glasa*, to the right of the old road at Skeabost Hall, is said to be a pulpit from which he preached.

"*St Columba's island in the Snizort River just below the bridges in Skeabost, is undoubtedly the most significant historical site in Skye. Its significance lies in the extent to which the rise and fall of this ecclesiastical complex depended on national and international politics.*"

So wrote Dr Alasdair Maclean, brother of the late poet Dr Sorley Maclean, and **the** expert on the history of this site.

From Norwegian documents of the 11th Century, we learn that it was then the seat of the Bishop of Skye, also called, the Bishop of Sodor. (The Sudereys were the Southern or Western Isles as opposed to the Nordereys. Orkney and Shetland.) This Bishopric was subject to the Archdiocese of Trondheim.

The first such Bishop of Skye was Wymund or Hamun, consecrated in 1079 at York.

Following the Battle of Largs in 1263, Norse influence in Skye began to wane, and by 1266 Skye was liberated from Norse rule after a period of some 400 years. With the departure of the invaders, power came to MacDonald Lord of the Isles. He reigned supreme until 1491 when the Kings of Scotland succeeded in breaking the power chain. The Lordship of the Isles now rests with the British heir to the throne. Prince Charles, Prince of Wales, is also Duke of Rothesay and Lord of the Isles. The importance of Snizort, under the patronage of the Lords of the Isles, can be seen in the fact that in 1428 Angus MacDonald, son of the chief, and cousin of King James I of Scotland was appointed Bishop of Snizort. With his father's support he was able to defy papal authority, his father threatening to remove the treasures from the Abbey of Iona. These treasures could well have ended up in Snizort if agreement had not been reached with the Benedictines. St. Columba's continued as the seat of the Bishops of the Isles until 1498, when it was moved to Iona.

The Cathedral at Snizort was a small one; the nave and chancel combined measure only 80feet. It may never have been intended as a permanent one. Bishop William Russel considered that the Isle of Man still lay in his Episcopal jurisdiction, and in 1499 hoped that the Isle of Man would be recovered from England. The present Anglican Bishopric is styled Sudor and Man.

It is said that the Cathedral was vacated in 1695, possibly as a result of erosion of the island by the river.

In the south transept can be seen a high relief of a knight in armour. This slab belonged to the MacSwan or MacSween family. Outside the North transept there is a damaged slab with a representation of Madonna and Child.

The other building of importance, to the west of the Cathedral proper, is better preserved. Known as Nicolson's Aisle, this is believed to be the burial place of 28 chiefs, or chief men, of Clan Nicolson, Skye's oldest clan. It is probably contemporary with the 11th Century Cathedral, as the Nicolsons are believed to have come to Skye around 950 AD.

Within the Cemetery are also to be found the graves of three generations of MacQueen ministers of Snizort. The Rev. Archibald MacQueen's headstone is believed to be part of an arch from the Cathedral. Donald MacQueen and Donald Munro, noted lay preachers of the 18th century, are also buried here. Donald Munro was known as the blind fiddler and was born at Achtalean, near Achachork on the outskirts of Portree.

Near to this spot is the site of the Battle of Trotternish in 1528 between the MacDonald and MacLeod clans. The battlefield, on what is now the Skeabost Golf Course, is called *Achadh na Fala*, the Field of Blood. It is said that the severed heads of the corpses were disposed of in the river and collected in a pool still known as *Coire nan Ceann*, the Cauldron of the Heads. This battle decided, once and for all, the ownership of Trotternish. Donald Gorm MacDonald defeated the MacLeods. Therafter, the Snizort River became the boundary between MacDonald and MacLeod territories.

It is interesting that this river also keeps back the predation of moles! These little creatures are not native to Skye, but were said to have been introduced by Lord Napier of Magdala when soil was imported for the gardens of Lyndale House. So far, they are confined to the west of the Snizort River.

Tote Stone

This is one of three Pictish Symbol stones to have been found in Skye. They provide evidence that the Picts occupied the island in early times. All three have the crescent and a V-rod symbols but this one also shows a double disc, Z-rod and mirror and comb. Both rods have floriated ends. Of the other two stones, one is at Dunvegan and the third was removed to the Royal Museum in Edinburgh, having been discovered on the beach at Fiscavaig.

Norse names abound in south Snizort. Several end in -shadder - from *setr* meaning shieling, and *bost* - from *bolstad-hir* meaning farm.

Close to here is the birthplace of Skye's famous bardess Mary MacPherson, *Mairi Mhor nan Oran,* big Mary of the Songs. Born in 1821, most of her poems extol the beauty of our native island but, her political poems spoke out on behalf of the people who were being exiled by a class who cared little about their oppression. Her book of Gaelic poetry contains nine thousand lines of verse, all dictated from memory, since, like the majority of ordinary folk born in the early nineteenth century, she had limited writing skills.

Her words against some of the ministers who failed to help the people in their dispute with Captain Fraser at Kilmuir, were strong:

> "*Weren't they the careless pastors,*
> *that kept their mouths so closed,*
> *Seeing the race of the brave worthies,*
> *Being scourged out of their parishes.*"

CHAPTER 19

Portree

Skye's present day capital was originally the village of Kiltaraglen (cell of Talorgan, an Irish saint) and was a mere cluster of houses when King James V landed at the Black Rock in 1540. He chose this spot as neutral territory between the MacLeod and MacDonald lands, and was entertained at Scorrybreak House by the Nicolson Chief. The King held Court in what is now the main square, Somerled Square. All the Chiefs and Nobles came to sware their allegiance. Thereafter the name of the town became Port Righ, Portree (the King's Harbour).

Until the 1750s, there were few houses around the bay, still known as St Columba's. St Columba's Island is opposite the Aros Centre, close to the shore at Penifiler. It was Sir James MacDonald of Sleat, the 8th baronet, born 1741, who laid out a very ambitious plan for the town. Sir James was a truly remarkable man, contemporary and friend of Adam Smith, and with a great aptitude for languages. His death, at the early age of 25, was a great blow to Clan Donald and indeed to the Isle of Skye. Sir James' outstanding abilities suggested parallels with the adopted son of Octavius Caesar, and so he has been called *"the Scottish Marcellus"*.

Most of the early streets of Portree were named after the aristocratic spouses of the MacDonald chiefs. (Douglas Row, Bosville Terrace, Beaumont Crescent and Wentworth Street.). Somerled Square was named after the great progenitor of Clan Donald who had a Celtic father and Norse mother. The Gaelic equivalent of the name Somerled is *Somhairle*, anglicised to Sorley. Some historians claim that the name, Somerled was the

Norse *sumar-lidi* meaning summer traveller or Viking. Somerled was Prince of Argyle and married Ragnhildis, daughter of Olaf the Red, King of Man in 1140. From this marriage sprung the dynasty of the Lords of the Isles.

The *Meall* or Lump, where the annual Skye Games are held, on the second Wednesday of August, was laid out by the Doctor Ban. He also built the round tower overlooking the harbour. This is the site of the last hanging in Skye. Angus Buchanan, one of the Packman murderers, was hanged *"with the greatest decency and without the least disturbance"*.

Meall House, once the local jail and the oldest building in Portree, now houses the offices of *Feisan na Gaidheal*, dedicated to the promotion of the Gaelic language and Highland Culture.

The old pier was another example of the work of the prolific Sir Thomas Telford. Although upgraded over the years, this area is now in need of major refurbishment.

As might be expected, the Scottish Episcopal Church in Portree is known as St. Columba's. In it is a memorial window in memory of Flora MacDonald. The subject of the window is *"Esther delivering her countrymen"*. The immortal words, *"If I perish, I perish"*, do indeed seem appropriate.

On the roof of the Aros Centre, there is a video-camera which monitors the wildlife around Portree Bay and St. Columba's Island. Grey seals, and, not-so-common Common seals, can be viewed in the Aros exhibition room, along with live views of the White-tailed Eagle eyrie and other nests in season. Birds from the Viewfield heronry are frequently seen on the foreshore as they spear butterfish and amphibians.

By the A87 road, now enclosed in the Glen Varagill forestry plantation, are the ruins of the 17th century home of a man famed for his physical strength and mental abilities. *Aodh Mor Maccuinn,* or Taog (like the Irish Taig) MacQueen was a man of great common sense who soon became famed for his clear and just views. He was often in demand when difficult questions arose, and when there were disputes which could not be solved by the usual means, Taog's judgements were regarded as final. On one occasion, he was called upon to judge between two Portree men who had a controversy. The two had been fishing off the rocks at Scorr on a very stormy evening. A large wave had washed one man into the sea. His companion, in casting his line to rescue him, had caught him in the eye with his hook and had thus pulled him to shore. As a result of this incident, the man had lost his eye and took his neighbour to court. Taog's judgement was in the same league as Solomon's. He suggested that they wait until the next, equally severe storm, and that the victim should be plunged into the sea at the same point. If he managed to swim ashore without assistance, he would receive damages for the loss of his eye. The complainant promptly dropped the case!

Across the Varagill river there is a narrow bridge called *Drochaid Mharshal*. On one particular dark night in the late 1800s, a local Braes man came upon a large and powerful highland bull blocking his way on the bridge. Completely unflustered, he seized the bull by the horns and twisted so that the angry beast fell into the river.

The Braes

The townships of the Braes of Trotternish are Camustianavaig, Conordan, Achnahanaid, Ollach, Gedintailor, Balameanach and Peinchorran. The last three of these had traditional grazing rights on Ben Lee, on Lord MacDonald's estate. In 1877 these rights were leased for sheep pasture to a tenant, John MacKay, who offered more rent for the privilege than the Braes crofters could afford. Having witnessed the success of the Valtos crofters in forcing a rent reduction, the Braes men approached the estate factor with a similar request, since they no longer had the means to pay. They were met with refusal and worse. No longer would a crofter be permitted to keep a dog. Wood for house-building could no longer be cut on the MacDonald Estate without payment, and thatching material for their homes could only be gathered if the factor's permission was first granted. Matters had reached a very serious pitch. Some peacemakers in the community persuaded the crofters to club together and offer more money if their rights were restored. Lord MacDonald said no! Many of the local men were employed in the fishing trade and regularly went to the south of Ireland in their open sailing boats. Here they encountered the Irish Land Leaguers. Charles Stewart Parnell had introduced the idea of 'boycotting' and had thus given the English language a new word. The effectiveness of this tactic had led to Parliament passing the Irish Land Act, which gave security of tenure and legally determined rents. The men of Braes wished for the same. Some decided to refuse to pay their rents to Lord MacDonald.

Inevitably the sheriff's officer was sent out to serve summonses on the offenders. They were to be removed from their crofts. The local people gathered, took the papers from him, and ceremonially burnt them on the road. This was viewed as the serious crime of "deforcement" and Sheriff William Ivory of Inverness felt that it had to be dealt with, quickly and effectively, before others in the Highlands began to act like Irish rebels. He summoned 50 policemen from Glasgow to ensure that the Braes crofters were brought to book. When they arrived on the MacBrayne's steamer 'Clansman' at Portree, they set off early for Braes with the Sheriff at their head. The weather, that morning of 19th April 1882, was miserable, with heavy rain and wind. On reaching Gedintailor, the crofters were rudely awakened. A warning message, however, was soon passed to the neighbouring townships, but not quickly enough to prevent the arrest of five men. Their purpose accomplished, the squad set off back towards Portree. At *Cuaig* the road narrows so that there is a sheer cliff to the right and a steep hill to the left. This was an ideal place for ambush. Although many of the men were away at sea, their women folk rose to the challenge and set upon the 50 strong police force with sticks, stones and peats. Although the Braes folk were outnumbered, their forceful stand gave needed ammunition to a group of newspaper reporters, who had travelled to witness the 'rebellion'. The general public of Britain were given the truth of the grim treatment that their crofter brethren had been suffering at the hands of the landlords. Sympathy was widespread. As a direct result of this *"the last battle on British soil"*, the Prime Minister, Gladstone, set up a Royal Commission to look into the crofters' grievances throughout the Highlands. Meanwhile, the five crofters were convicted and fined at Inverness. Their fines were paid by the citizens of that town and they were feted and brought back home as heroes.

By October of 1882, the Braes crofters had negotiated a rent reduction and had their rights to Ben Lee restored.

Mairi Mhor did not fail to satirise Sheriff Ivory but likened him to Judas Iscariot: *"A grey stone will certainly be placed above you, which will record your iniquitous bribes, and how you sold your entire reputation for a little booty, for the sake of your corrupt ground, exactly like Judas."*

Napier Commission

In the spring of 1883 the Government announced its intention to set up a Royal Commission 'to inquire into the condition of the crofters and cottars in the Highlands and Islands of Scotland'. Not long afterwards, on the 8th of May, the Napier Commission had its first meeting to hear crofters' grievances. It was significant that the commission first met here in Braes at the Ollach Church and schoolhouse. After a year of such meetings throughout the North of Scotland, a report was published which led to the Crofters' Holding Act of 1886. This was by no means the end of the crofters' troubles but peace would soon come. In 1897, the Government appointed Congested Districts Board, began to alleviate some of the longstanding problems that the people were experiencing.

Since these times, the lot of crofters has seen many changes, most of them undoubtedly for the better. The definition of crofter as agreed by the Napier Commission was: 'a small tenant of the land with or without a lease, who finds in the cultivation and produce of his holding a material portion of his occupation, earnings and sustenance, and who pays rent to the proprietor.'

A more cynical modern definition of a croft might be:

'*A small area of land surrounded by red tape*".

Farewell to Trotternish

Our visit to the Braes area brings our **virtual** tour of Trotternish to an end. I trust that, if you have enjoyed the book, you will soon make a personal visit to the Isle of Skye so that you can undertake an **actual** tour. Hopefully these tales have acted as a stimulus, and you too will soon be enchanted by the atmosphere, the peace and the tranquillity which make this island such a wonderful place in which to live and to visit.

Beannachd leat!

So when was that then?

AD 585   First visit by St. Columba to Skye

700   Adamnan's book: Life of St. Columba

1263   Battle of Largs. Norse under King Haakon defeated.

1265   Treaty of Perth. King Magnus gives up claim to Scottish Isles. Lords of the Isles take control of Skye after the Norse leave.

1493   Lordship of the Isles ends.

1528   Battle of Trotternish

1540   King James V visits Skye.

1601   Last Clan Battle at Coire na Creiche.

1651   Skye's first school at Shulista

1703   Martin Martin: Description of the Western Isles of Scotland.

1715   The Old Pretender's Rebellion

1722   Flora MacDonald born at Milton South Uist.

1745   The Young Pretender's Rebellion

1746   Culloden. "Over the Sea to Skye".

1748   Disarming Act. No more wearing of tartan or carrying arms.

1770   Beginnings of Emigration to South Carolina.

1773   Johnson and Boswell at Kingsburgh.

1790   Death of Flora MacDonald

1792   Death of Dr. John MacLean at Shulista

1824   Kilmuir loch drained.

1843   Disruption of the Scottish Kirk.

1882   Battle of the Braes.

1886   The Crofters' Holding Act.

Bibliography

Cameron, A	*The History and Traditions of The Isle of Skye*	1871	Inverness
Cooper, D	*Skye*	1970	London
Hunter, J and MacLean, C	*Skye: The Island*	1986	Edinburgh
Johnson, S	*A Journey to the Western Isles of Scotland*	1774	London
Kilmuir History & Heritage Group	*Kilmuir & Kilmaluag, North Skye: Echoes from the Past*	2006	Kilmuir
MacColl A. W.	*Land, Faith & The Crofting Community*	2006	Edinburgh
MacCulloch, J. A.	*The Misty Isle of Skye*	1905	Edinburgh
MacDonald, J	*Discovering Skye*	1982	Duntulm
MacDonald, J	*Flora Macdonald: Heroine of the Jacobite Cause*	1989	Duntulm
MacDonald, J	*A Short History of Crofting in Skye*	1998	Duntulm
MacGregor, A. A.	*Over the Sea to Skye*	1926	Edinburgh
MacGregor, J.	*In the Footsteps of Bonnie Prince Charlie*	1988	London
MacKenzie, W.	*Old Skye Folk Tales: Traditions, Reflections & Memories*	1933	Culnacnoc
MacSween, A	*Skye*	1990	Edinburgh
Martin Martin	*A Description of the Western Islands of Scotland*	1703	London
McMillan, R. L.	*Skye Birds*	2005	Elgol
Monro, Sir D.	*Description of the Western Isles of Scotland called Hybrides*	1774	Edinburgh
Murray, C. W and Birks	*The Botanist in Skye*	1974	Portree
Newton, N	*Skye*	1995	Newton Abbot

Nicolson, A.	1930	History of Skye	Glasgow
Sellar, W. D. H. and MacLean, A.	1999	The Highland Clan MacNeacail (MacNicol)	Waternish
Silver, F.	2006	The Skye Magazine	Stornoway
Smith, A	1865	A Summer in Skye	London
Stephenson, D. and Merritt, J.	2002	Skye: A Landscape fashioned by Geology	Edinburgh
Sterry, P and Press, B.	2004	Wildflowers of Britain and Europe	London
Swire, O. F.	1952	Skye: The Island and its Legends	Glasgow
Thomson, D. S.	1994	The Companion to Gaelic Scotland	Glasgow
Willis, D	1991	The Story of Crofting in Scotland	Edinburgh
Yoxon, P. and Yoxon, G.	1987	Guide to the Natural History of Skye	Broadford

Printed in the United Kingdom
by Lightning Source UK Ltd.
127095UK00001B/232-399/P